BERMUDA'S
TEA TIME TREATS
- for coffee lovers too!

By Mair L. D. Harris

BERMUDA'S TEA TIME TREATS

By Mair L. D. Harris

Dedicated to my parents, John and Pat Jones, who nurtured my love of cooking by sending me to college.

To my husband, Jack, who has continually encouraged me, and to our children, Mark and Kara, who served as first-class tasters.

Special thanks to Catherine, my editor, whose advice and friendship has been invaluable.

Lastly, thanks to Jonny Cunningham, the book's designer, who has made my very basic visual concept a splendid reality.

A tithe from sales of this book will be given to:
Learning Disabilities Association of Bermuda
New Tribes Mission, U.K.

Acknowledgements:
The Tea Council (U.K.)
Premier Brands (U.K.)
Robin Sigley (U.S.A.)
China: Mrs. Joan Moore private collection (BDA) & Mrs. T's Victorian Tearoom (BDA)
Photography courtesy of Mr. Kevin John Leask (U.K.) & the author, M.L.D. Harris
Cover: Teapot by Pelican Products (available in all quality stores throughout Bermuda)

EDITED BY
Catherine Harriott
Author: Maverick Guide to Bermuda, Pelican Books (www.pelicanpub.com)

DESIGNED BY
Jonathan & Susan Cunningham
JJinc Design®
Lincolnshire, ENGLAND
(07951) 070224
jonathan_cunningham@ntm.org.uk

Printed in Singapore
by Stamford Press Pte Ltd

PUBLISHED BY
Manna Publications
P.O. Box 157, Sandys, SB BX, Bermuda.
E-mail: teatime@northrock.bm

Foreword

Tea is my drink. Having spent almost my entire adult life in Bermuda, tea and the gracious art of teatime has become an established practise when entertaining friends. Friendships with women have flourished over a cuppa at their place or mine, or sometimes meeting at tea-rooms such as Mrs. T's Victorian Tea Room, or afternoon tea at the Waterloo House Hotel.

I remember well, as a young teacher in St. George's, stopping off with a colleague at the Castle Harbour Hotel, and taking tea and goodies while resting in the lobby's deep couches. Often at weekends we would meet for lunch at the old Tea Cosy on Burnaby Hill, Hamilton, or visit a hotel for afternoon tea at 4 o'clock. Sundays, we would journey by bus to Somerset and enjoy tea and syllabub at the Belfield Hotel.

Each year, on the Queen's Birthday public holiday, held in June, a traditional afternoon tea was served in the grounds of Government House for invited guests only. However, if you signed the visitors' book at the gate a few weeks prior to the event, an invitation would be duly sent. Carefully coifed and dressed in our best frocks, we would drive our somewhat old and battered car onto the grounds, enjoy the splendour of the gardens, taking tea with a wondrous assortment of fare by the pool.

As a home economics teacher, it was my duty to organise refreshments for any school function. On one occasion, Prize Day in 1969, I needed a large water urn to heat water for the tea. As the airport kitchen was close by, I called and asked the Production Manager if he could possibly loan me an urn for the afternoon. I duly picked it up, and, upon returning, met the manager to say thank you; it was from this meeting that some years later he became my husband.

Later on, in our life as a married couple, my husband became manager at one of the Island's hotels. It was my job, once a week, to serve afternoon tea from a silver service. It proved a nice way to meet the guests and sometimes we would invite a couple to our home for afternoon tea. Always baking my own items from scratch, I would serve scones, an assortment of cookies and cakes, as well as tea. We made lasting friendships from all over the world.

For many years I worked in the field of catering, organising all kinds of functions – anything from intimate gatherings of two guests, to banquets with hundreds of people as well as on-site catering for three movies shot in Bermuda. Indeed, I catered to a variety of tea parties; children's birthdays, tea parties on the beach, on board a paddle steamer, yacht, launching a new tug and at Camden (the Premier's official residence) just to name a few.

Nowadays, vacations in the mother country -- Britain -- are spent buying tea memorabilia, and enjoying tea in a variety of locales: high class teas in hotels such as the Waldorf; Devon and Cornish clotted cream teas; and tea in the parlour of an elderly lady in Beatrix Potter's home village in the Lake District.

Tea has been for me, not just a drink but a life experience. I hope it will be for you too. Join me for a cuppa sometime at E-mail teatime@northrock.bm.

Tea Time

Our Exclusive Bermuda Gifts
Double The Pleasure Of The Tea Time Ritual!

Bermuda Cottage Ceramic Cookie Jar • Bermuda Cottage Tea Cosy
Bermudiana Bone China Mini Tea Set And Cup & Saucer
Bermuda Flowers Linen Tea Towel
Bermuda Flowers Vinyl Coated Cotton Apron

Hamilton And Branch Shops Islandwide

TRIMINGHAM'S

BERMUDA

— SINCE 1842 —

Table of Contents

Page Number

1. The History of Tea 7

2. All About Tea 17

3. Island Talents 23

4. My Lords and Ladies 37

5. Recipes from around the World 51

6. Afternoon Tea around the Island 67

7. Best of British 81

8. High Tea 93

9. Especially for Kids 107

10. Coffee Lovers' Treats 117

11. Speciality Teas 133

Tea Equipage 145

Tea Trivia 149

Weights & Measures 153

Index 157

1

The History of Tea

Tea comes to Britain and America . . . 8

Everything Stops for Tea 9

Opium and other Wars 10

Afternoon Tea in Bermuda 10

(A NEW SONG on TEA) 11

"Tea is drunk to forget the din of the world" (T'ien Yiheng)

Legends are sometimes delightful, sometimes gruesome. The legends of tea's invention give us both varieties. The nicer type is the tale of a certain Chinese Emperor, Shen Nung (3000 BC), who, for purification purposes, was boiling a little water under a camellia tree. And, like many of us today who know a watched pot never boils, when Nung's attention was elsewhere, the breeze gently laid a leaf or two from the tree into the water. Shen Nung enjoyed the flavour of the first cup of tea.

A less enchanting tale comes to us again from the East, when a certain Buddhist Indian monk travelled to China. While deep in meditation he drifted off to sleep, but upon awakening, was so angered by his weakness, he cut off his eyelids. The legend says, where they fell, tea plants grew.

All legends aside, records show that wild tea was grown some 5,000 years ago, however, the first real mention of tea was in Ch'a Ching, Book of Tea (now known as The Classic Tea) written by Lu Yu (AD 780), during the Tang dynasty. Lu Yu's book taught the Chinese how to properly manufacture and brew tea, and he became known as the patron saint of tea.

The Chinese' green tea was pressed into blocks for transportation to eastern countries like Japan, where its use led to the evolution of the Japanese tea ceremony ritual, or Cha-no-yu. But it was not until the European shipping trading routes in the early 1600s that tea finally reached western shores. Dutch traders claim to be the first to bring back tea as cargo, with the Portuguese a close second. In 1615, the Chinese gave Russia a gift of tea: Camels carried tea chests overland, taking 18 months in the process, thus naming the famous Russian Caravan tea.

Tea comes to Britain and America

In 1658, the first advertisement for tea by Thomas Garraway, a merchant in London's Exchange Alley, read: "That excellent, and by all means physicians' approved, China Drink called by the Chinaceans, T'Cha."

Tea's chance at becoming accepted as an English aristocratic drink came when England's King, Charles II, married Portugal's Princess, Catherine of Braganza (1662). Part of this Princess's Portuguese dowry was a chest of tea (and the territories of Tangier and Bombay). The John Company, tea merchants, who later merged and was renamed the East India Company, used Tangier and Bombay as their base to China. With tea's growing popularity, the government of the day seized on the notion to impose heavy taxation. To avoid this duty, smuggling became rife and, to save money, polluted teas began springing up -- leaves mixed with other non-tea leaves and ash. As green teas were easier to pollute, the public began to turn to black tea for better quality control.

In 1717, an enterprising young man, Tom Twining, who already owned coffee shops for young men to meet, tapped into the ladies market by converting one of his coffee shops into the first tea shop: The Golden Lyon. Today, Twining teas are still popular.

Across the Atlantic in the new colony of America, tea had become popularised much to the same degree as in England, replacing gin and ale as the household drink. The East India Company held the tea monopoly on the Eastern Seaboards, and when the British government heavily taxed tea in 1767, the thirsty colonists were not at all pleased and began smuggling in tea from Holland. In the Tea Act of 1773, Britain granted the East India Company permission to cut out the American tea merchants and sell directly to the colonists. Angry Bostonians rebelled by tipping 342 chests of tea into Boston harbour, known as the famous Boston Tea Party. No storm in a teacup, this peaceful revolution was the precursor to the American War of Independence.

In 1784, the tax on tea was cut from 119% to 12.5%, and by the following century, tea had become the popular drink of all classes of people.

The Americans also have the distinction of inventing the tea bag and iced tea. America's first World Fair in 1904 saw trade exhibitors from around the world. One such exhibitor, Richard Blechynden, because of a heat wave, put ice into his tea and it was a huge success.

Another accidental discovery was the tea bag. In 1908, Thomas Sullivan of New York was a tea merchant who gave free bags of tea-taster samples to restaurants. He soon realised he was on to a good thing when he noticed they were brewing the tea in their bags.

Everything Stops for Tea

The very British tradition of afternoon tea was initiated by Anna, the 7th Duchess of Bedford, who, in 1840, apparently decided a little nibble mid-afternoon raised her spirits. So, during Queen Victoria's reign (1837-1901), all things tea: tea services, tea trays, tea gowns, and afternoon tea parties at

4 p.m. were well established amongst the aristocracy.

The men of the labouring classes welcomed high tea when, at the end of the working day, the family would sit around a table of hot and cold dishes as well as sweet fare of cake and pies.

Opium and other Wars

While the ladies of the Manor were sipping tea and nibbling cakes at their little afternoon parties, the English had the devilish plan of paying the Chinese for their tea in addictive opium. For 50 years the East India Company grew opium in India, and tea was traded in this loathsome manner. The Opium Wars (1840-1842) between the British and the Chinese led to the 158-year colonisation of Hong Kong by the British.

During Europe's two World Wars there was vigilant rationing and tea was a precious commodity; a hardship to a nation of tea drinkers where tea now had a firm stronghold on British taste buds. Subsequent years have seen the popularity of tea go from strength-to-strength with variety teas becoming fashionable.

Afternoon Tea in Bermuda

Juan de Bermudez discovered Bermuda in 1503. But it was after a shipwreck in 1609, in which Sir George Somers and 150 survivors lived to tell the tale, that it was colonised by the British. The first immigrants arrived in 1612 aboard The Plough, and a little later green tea began its migration from east to west. However, it seems that in Bermuda it had not yet reached a drink of any popularity. Henry Wilkinson in his book Bermuda in the Old Empire, quotes from Governor, Sir Robert Robinson, in 1687: "Fish, potatoes and a sort of loblolly made from Indian corn are the chief food of the people, while their general drink is Adam's ale." He goes on to say, "Only in Queen Anne's time did tea and coffee commence to rival it on one hand and ardent spirits on the other."

As the first weekly newspaper, The Gazette, only began in 1784, and the first Customs entries, available in the Bermuda archives, commenced in 1792, it is somewhat difficult to estimate the extent of tea or coffee drinking in the interim period. We can only think that like the rest of the Western Hemisphere, tea and coffee had become popular beverages, taking over ale and gin as the household drink.

Wilkinson does tell us that when 10,000 pounds worth of tea was tossed into Boston harbour in 1773, news of this violence of the Bostonians reached Bermuda by way of the West Indies. Henry Tucker, a prominent member of society in Bermuda, writing to his brother-in-law in Virginia, wrote, "I am as attached to liberty as any man but I cannot say I like their proceedings." Mr. Tucker felt the Americans could have instead declined to buy tea.

An early Customs entry, details that on 4th December, 1792, 10 casks of coffee, 12 bags of cocoa, and 2 bushels of sugar were imported from Jamaica along with salt from the Turks and Caicos Islands. Indeed, from Customs entries during that time, supplies seem to have been imported from many of the West Indian Islands: sugar from Dominica, ginger from Barbados, molasses from St. Vincent. Flour came in from America.

On 6th September, 1794, 170 bags of tea and 149 casks of coffee were brought into the Island, under, what seems to be unhappy circumstances. The Bill of Lading noting, "The voyage from Curacao put into this port in distress for want of water and injuries suffered in a gale of wind." As the Brigadoon was American, he possibly had set sail from the West Indies for American shores when a diversion to Bermuda was required.

The Gazette gives us insight into habits of the day, and on the front page of the very first edition, 17th January 1784, is this poem:

A NEW SONG on TEA

Teach me, ye Nine, to sing of tea,
Of grateful Green, of black Bohea.
Hark! the Kettle softly singing
How again it bubbles o'er;
Quickly, John, Black Susan bring in,
Water in the Teapot pour.

The Bread and Butter thinly slice,
Oh spread it delicately nice;
Let the Toast be crisp and crumpling,
The Cakes as doughy as a Dumpling:
The eating, fipping, snuffing up the Steam,
We chat, and, 'midst a motley chaos seem-
Of Cups and Saucers, Butter, Bread and Cream.

Tea accoutrements were certainly imported along with tea. In the Historical Society Museum, we find a late 18th century tea caddy on display, and in St. George's a teapot, probably from the same era, with a John Wesley motto:

We thank thee Lord for this our food
But more because of Jesus blood.
Let manna to our Souls be given
The bread of life sent down from heaven.

It was in this century that John Wesley's followers had disapproved of tea as a wicked drink.

By the late 1800s, Mrs. Hallet, in her writings of the diary, Rosabelle, Life in Bermuda in the 19th Century, tells of "an Old Fashioned Tea Drinkage," organised by Rosabelle and friends and hosted by Governor Laffan -- 30 pounds sterling was raised for "relief for the deserving poor of the community."

In the 20th century, the aristocracy started visiting Bermuda to avoid North America's frigid winters. As tourism flourished, hotels were built and the tradition of afternoon tea was firmly established. In the 1920s at the hotel, Bermudiana, afternoon tea concerts were held in the lounge between 4 and 5 p.m., and tea was served every afternoon "on the lounge and terraces." At the Princess Hotel (named after Princess Louise, Queen Victoria's daughter), Tea Dansants with the hotel orchestra were popular. Among the attractions advertised at Elba (now known as Elbow) Beach Hotel on the South Shore, were bathing, tennis, afternoon tea, dinner and dancing.

Before the end of the century, tennis was introduced into Bermuda, and then onto the United States. The European tradition of tennis tea parties was also carried on, well into the next century. In the Bermudian Cookbook, Miss Gladys Hutching -- the first Bermudian to play Wimbledon -- tells of a typical tennis tea party of the 1920s:

> The players (10-12) arrived about 2.30 p.m., some on bicycles [cars were not allowed until 1947] others in carriages. The ladies were always dressed in white with coloured sweaters and lovely homespun coats to match. The men wore long white flannels. About 4.30 p.m. everyone was invited to have tea around the dining table, which was beautifully set with flowers matching the teaset. What a spread! Sandwiches galore (nut or brown bread), hot biscuits or Johnny cake, cookies, layer cakes (lemon, orange, chocolate, coconut) [Bermuda's humid climate is said to be good for making layer cakes]. Many cups of tea were consumed; the men usually had up to six. This was a wonderful way of entertaining.

Tea-rooms spread all over the Island: The Little Green Door Tea Garden in

Hamilton opened its doors in 1910. Also in Hamilton, Judith Watson tells us in her booklet, Bermuda: Traditions and Tastes, there was Kitty Darrell's Tea-Room and The Goody Shop on Reid Street. Going west was Claudia Darrell's Waterlot Inn, Jenny Fowle's Old Post Office Tea-Room and White Swan Tea House. Going east was Miss Stephenson's Tea Garden in Flatts Village and The Bluebird Tea-Room in Bailey's Bay, while the old St. George's Hotel housed the Snow Plant Tea-Room. In later years, she fondly remembers The Captain's Cabin on Pitt's Bay Road, The Tea Cosy in Hamilton, and Belfield in Somerset.

Ms. Watson spins a favourite tale of Kate Tucker, the owner of The Little Green Door Tea Garden, said to be Mark Twain's favourite tea-room. Tucker ran her tea-room from 1910 to 1938, and was the subject of a little scandal when she was summoned to court for advertising by way of a flag (Bermuda used to have nothing better to do in those halcyon days). She defeated the courts by changing her flag's teapot sign to a letter "T" which, she claimed, stood for her name and therefore was a house flag, which was within the law. The American press picked up the story, one Boston newspaper declaring it: "A Second Tea Party."

As tourism grew and hotels were built, the tradition of afternoon tea at 4 p.m. continued for visitors, who, after a day of sightseeing or lazing on the beach, enjoyed this repast to tide them over until dinner at 8 p.m. For residents of Bermuda, however, life became busier. Women were in the workforce, wartime intervened, and afternoon tea had less of a place.

Traditions have ways of enduring, especially in islands where the life is more insular. Bermuda's churches still play host to fairs and tea parties, as do clubs for seniors, like The Joy Club in St. George's. Many hotels continue with traditional afternoon tea at 4 p.m. Renewed interest in tea and the art of teatime has brought about tea-rooms such as Mrs. T's Victorian Tea-Room in Southampton and the Lighthouse Tea-Rooms in the old lighthouse keeper's cottage below Gibbs Hill Lighthouse.

***

For 5,000 years, tea has been an important part of the traditions of the East and West, and is currently enjoying a resurgence, thanks in part to studies proving tea's medicinal value. But many of us care only about tea's enjoyment. As Lu t'ung, a Chinese poet during the Tang dynasty, said in AD 780: "I am in no way interested in immortality but only in the taste of tea."

To be S O L D

On the most reasonable Terms

By Mrs Stockdale, at Saint George's

Best single, refined

LOAF SUGAR, very hard.

Best Hyson Tea,

20s per lb.

A small quantity of exceeding Fine scented HAIR POWDER, In quarter pound, half pound and Pound papers at 3s 4d. per lb.

Goucester and double Gloucester CHEESE

Rice of the best Quality

To be S O L D

EDWARD DUNSCOMBE, at Pitt's Bay, in the Lane Imported in the sloop HOPE,

FLOUR,

RUM,

Sugar in Barrels

Cordage of different sizes

Canvas from No 1 to 4

JUST IMPORTED,

In the Sloop LADY HAM-MOND PACKET

And to be sold by G.Muir and Co.

SUPERFINE FLOUR.

Ship bread.

Linseed oil.

Shell Almonds.

Barley in Kegs.

Best Dumb Fish.

Soap.

Candles.

Cheese.

Paints.

Spices.

Best Hyson Tea.

A few barrels excellent Cyder.

St. George's, May 1

Just opened, a chest of fresh Hyson TEA, of a superior Quality and flavour, and to be sold At 20s. per pound by

MARTHA COX

CEYLINDO

"A PERFECT TEA"

Awarded the

ONLY GOLD MEDAL

For Imported Teas at the SOUTH AFRICAN EXHIBITION Grahamstown, Conclusively proving it to be the

PREMIER TEA

OF THEWORLD

AT GOSLING BROS.

A LARGE STOCK OF THE

FINEST GROCERIES

ENGLISH LOAF SUGAR

Mocha and Java Coffee

always freshly roasted

Souchong, Hyson, Oolong And Congon Teas

THE BRAND CEYLON TEAS

(awarded Gold Medal at Chicago) especially packed at the Gardens for the above.

1900

New Goods

CONSISTING OF:

JAPANESE CHINA TEA SETS, Cups and saucers, Dishes, Salad bowls, Vases, Flower pots, Inlaid tea trays, Table tops, Baskets, etc., (Also a few Japanese, Indian and Turkish Silk and Satin Table Covers — very cheap)

Table cutlery in ivory and celluloid handles, Knives and forks from 5/ doz. Up

Best make of Coal Stoves and Ranges, Oil stoves, Heaters and Gas Stoves

Expected Per Next TRINIDAD

EATHERN WARE and CHINA—Consisting of: Tea Breakfast and Dinner Sets, in all qualities.

H.C. MASTERS.

Hamilton, Bda.

1921

South Shore Hotel

Overlooking Bermuda's Most Famous Sand Beach

Bathing Parties	Shore Dinner
Afternoon Teas	Strawberries and Cream

Comfortable and Commodious Conveyance

Leaves Queen Street, Hamilton

10 a.m.   1 p.m.   2.30 & 5 p.m.

2

All About Tea

Tea Growing 18

Fruit and Herbal Infusions 19

A Good Cup of Tea 20

Tea Growing

The botanical name for the teaplant is Camellia Sinensis. The teabush can grow up to 40-50 feet, though is kept pruned for easy plucking. The leaves are dark green, rather like those of a privet hedge, with small white blossoms.

Grown in tropical or sub-tropical areas, sometimes at great altitudes, the main tea producing countries are India, China, Africa, Indonesia, Sri Lanka, Taiwan, Japan, Turkey and Russia. Climate, altitude and latitude influence the type of tea grown.

Tea is grown commercially on plantations, estates or gardens of varying sizes. Rows and rows of chest-height bushes cover the land. Careful plucking of the young leaves and bud is still done by hand and put into baskets or bags carried on the back or heads of the pluckers. Full baskets are then transported to factories, which are often on the larger estates.

For the production of green tea, leaves are sun-dried and then fired. However, black tea is dried, rolled and fermented before being fired. Oolong teas are semi-fermented. Scented teas are made with additions such as jasmine flowers. Fruit flavoured teas have fruit oils blended into the finished tea. Speciality teas may be a special blend of teas from a certain area, or from various areas but with definite characteristics.

The tea estate labels the tea with country of origin and whether it is a broken or whole leaf tea. Nowadays, tea is packaged in sacks, rather than tea chests, then it's on to the auction where Tea Blenders taste, bid for, and ship to the purchasing company's headquarters.

Once the tea reaches the manufacturer, it is either packaged for the consumer as a single-leaf tea or, more usually, made into a blend. Thirty different teas might be required for one blend. Once a blend acquires a name, it must always taste the same.

The British Tea Council gives us these suggestions for teas that you may find on your supermarket or speciality store shelves:

Type	Country of Origin	Brewing Time	Milk/Black/ Lemon	Characteristics
Darjeeling	India	3-5 mins.	Black or Milk	Delicate, slightly astringent flavour
Assam	India	3-5 mins.	Black or Milk	Full bodied, with a rich, smooth, malty flavour
Ceylon	Sri Lanka	3-5 mins.	Black or Milk	Brisk, full flavour, with a bright colour
Kenya	Kenya (Africa)	2-4 mins.	Black or Milk	Strong with brisk flavour
Earl Grey	China	3-5 mins.	Black or Lemon	Citrus bergamot flavoured
Lapsang Souchong	China	3-5 mins.	Black	Smoky aroma and flavour
Oolong	Oolong (China)	5-7 mins.	Black	Subtle, delicate, lightly flavoured

Fruit and Herbal Infusions

Fruit teas sold are blackcurrant, grapefruit, mandarin, lime, and raspberry, to name a few. Herbal ones like camomile, ginseng, spearmint, and spiced ones like ginger, orange and honey are on supermarket as well as health food store shelves. These are not usually made with Camellia Sinensis leaves but with a leaf such as hibiscus. As healthy life-styles gain credence, herbal teas are also drunk for holistic remedies.

A Good Cup of Tea

Here's the Tea Council's advice on brewing a good cuppa:

- Use a good quality loose leaf or bagged tea (stored in airtight container at room temperature).
- Always use freshly drawn boiling water (previously boiled water loses oxygen).
- Measure the tea carefully: Use 1 tea bag or 1 rounded teaspoon of loose tea for each cup to be served.
- Allow the tea to brew for recommended time before pouring.

Note: Many people suggest that warming the pot first is the secret to a good cup of tea.

So hear it then, my
  Rennie dear,
Nor hear it with a
  frown:
Thou cannot make
  the tea so fast
As I can gulp it
  down.

I therefore pray thee,
  Rennie dear,
That thou wilt give
  to me
With cream and
  sugar softened well,
Another dish of tea.
  Dr. Samuel Johnson (1709-1784)

3

Island Talents

Bermuda's tiny spot in the ocean belies the multitude of her talented cooks. Cosmopolitan by nature, being in-between two continents, her heritage of tasty delights is equally as diverse. This chapter's recipes capture some of Bermuda's special cultural diversity.

Johnny Bread 24

Gingerbread 25

Dream Bars 26

Melt-in-the-Mouth Cookies 28

Hyacinth's Tea Cakes 29

Sugar Cookies 30

Cream Cheese and
Tinned Shrimp Sandwiches 31

Cream Puffs 32

Double Lemon Shortbread 34

Tomato Jam 35

INGREDIENTS:

2 cups all purpose flour
4 teaspoons baking powder
¼ teaspoon salt
2 tablespoons sugar
4 tablespoons shortening
   or lard
½ — ¾ cup milk

Type of Pan:

Griddle or heavy frying pan

Cooking Temperature:

Low/moderate

Cooking Time:

20 — 25 minutes

Alternative Ingredients:

For a high tea, add grated cheese to mixture.

Secret Touch:

For a different taste, replace 1 cup of flour with 1 cup of cornmeal.

Anecdote:

Johnny Bread or "Journey Bread" is an old standby from way back. Stephen Dean of Dean's Bakery in Somerset, sells about 100 a day and says it is very popular with tourists.

Johnny Bread
by Sarah Bea Hayward

In the old town of St. George's, Sarah worked in service (as they called it in years gone by) for over ten years. As was the custom in many wealthy Bermudian homes, afternoon tea was served with their finest silver and best bone china at four o'clock. At tennis parties, Sarah would have to haul the china and silver the long trek to the courts.

This is Sarah's recipe for Johnny Bread, a time-honoured Bermudian favourite. Johnny Bread looks like a large scone or tea biscuit and tastes delicious warm from the griddle, spread with jam.

Method:

1. Sift all dry ingredients into a mixing bowl. Add shortening and rub together with fingertips until mixture resembles fine breadcrumbs.

2. Initially, add ½ cup milk and mix to soft dough; add more milk if required.

3. Knead dough on a lightly floured board until smooth. Form into a round shape, 1" thick.

4. Preheat a griddle or lightly greased frying pan. Keep stove ring heat low to moderate and cook until golden brown on each side — about 10 — 12 minutes each side.

Gingerbread

by Joy Fubler

Even though Joy is busy with her church and community work, she still finds time to entertain. Along with husband Ivan, she cooks and hosts many cosy gatherings at their home.

Try her mouth-watering recipe for Gingerbread.

Method:

1. Preheat oven, grease and flour pan.

2. In a mixing bowl, mix together oil, sugar, molasses, and a *little* of the boiling water.

3. Add dry ingredients and rest of water.

4. Bake until a skewer comes out clean.

5. Remove from oven, cool 10 minutes in pan and turn out.

INGREDIENTS:

1 cup cooking oil
1 cup sugar
1 cup molasses
2 cups boiling water
4 cups all purpose flour
2 tablespoons cinnamon
2 tablespoons ginger
4 tablespoons baking soda

Type of Pan:

11½" x 9½" deep pan
(lightly greased and floured)

Baking Temperature:

350°F

Baking Time:

1¼ — 1½ hours

Alternative Ingredients:

1 cup raisins, 1 teaspoon vanilla essence.

Secret Touch:

This easy recipe is perfect for a party, school, or church function.

Anecdote:

Bermudians are famous for working long past retirement. Joy's mother, a professional cook — or Aunt Mattie as she was known — retired at 82, only to be enticed back by her employers for another two years!

Dream Bars
by Tracey Caswell

INGREDIENTS:

Base

1 cup all purpose flour
2 tablespoons confectioner's
  sugar
½ cup butter

Topping

2 eggs
1 cup brown sugar
¼ cup flour
⅛ teaspoon salt
1 teaspoon baking powder
1 teaspoon vanilla essence
1 cup chopped walnuts
1 cup coconut

Type of Pan:

8" square pan (greased)

Baking Temperature:

300°F

Baking Time:

20 minutes for base, then
another 30 minutes
with topping

---

*Better to be deprived of
food for three days, than
tea for one.*

Ancient Chinese
Proverb

Tracey is the author of Tea with Tracey:
The Woman's Survival Guide to Living in
Bermuda — a practical, entertaining guide
to coping in paradise.

Born in Canada she came to Bermuda
many years ago with her Bermudian
husband, and has learned, over the years,
the little tips for living in her sub-tropical
island home. Her book is a must-have for
new residents or anyone thinking of
moving to a warmer climate. Tracey shares
this shortbread recipe with luscious
topping – a Canadian favourite, which, she
assures us, adapts to the humid climate.

Method:

Base

1. Preheat oven, grease pan.

2. In a mixing bowl, mix flour and
   confectioner's sugar.

3. Blend in butter with a pastry blender
   or your fingers until it resembles
   fine breadcrumbs.

4. Pat firmly in pan and bake for
   20 minutes.

Topping

1. In a mixing bowl, beat eggs well;
   add sugar.

2. Stir together flour, salt, and baking
   powder; blend into egg mixture.

3. Add vanilla, nuts, and coconut.

4. Spread over cooked base.

5. Bake again for 30 minutes. Allow to cool until fully cold, then cut into squares or bars and remove from pan.

Secret Touch:

Topping is very soft when first removed from oven but becomes firm as it cools.

Anecdote:

Tracey's favourite saying for those who are trying to keep their house spick and span in Bermuda's humid climate:

> Keep it Clean–
> Keep it Dry–
> Keep it Moving–
> Keep it Cold.

Come share my pot of tea,
My house is warm and
my friendship's free.
Author unknown

WILLIAM SHAKESPEARE 1564 - 1616

Melt-in-the-Mouth Cookies

by Linda Cox

INGREDIENTS:

½ cup softened butter or
   margarine
1 cup light brown sugar
1 egg
1 teaspoon vanilla essence
¾ cup all purpose flour
1 teaspoon baking powder
½ teaspoon salt
½ cup chopped walnuts,
   almonds, or pecans

Type of Pan:

Cookie sheets (ungreased)

Baking Temperature:

400°F

Baking Time:

5 minutes

Secret Touch:

When baked, scoop off pan
quickly before they harden,
or they will be difficult
to remove.

Anecdote:

Linda recalls fond memories
of her Gramma Pierce, always
in an apron, always cooking
from scratch. Every week,
Gramma baked with apples
from the apple orchard in
their family's five-acre farm,
filling the house with their
sweet aroma.

Linda is a trained dietician who currently works alongside her husband Wil at Miles Market Grocery and Speciality Gourmet Store. She and Wil relish cooking together, and this superb cookie recipe came from her American Grandmother, Gramma Pierce, who hailed from Upper Saddle River, New Jersey.

Method:

1. Preheat oven.

2. In a mixing bowl, cream together butter and sugar until light and fluffy; add egg and vanilla.

3. Sift in flour, baking powder, and salt. Stir in chopped nuts.

4. Drop dollops of ½ teaspoonfuls of mixture onto cookie sheets. Space out well.

5. Bake for 5 minutes, keeping an eye on them all the time.

Makes 30 — 40 cookies.

Hyacinth's Tea Cakes

by Hyacinth Roberts

During the 1800s, after the abolition of slavery, many people from the Portuguese islands were brought to Bermuda to work on the land. Many stayed, and their children and grandchildren became lawyers, doctors, politicians and businessmen. Like many Bermudians today, Hyacinth Roberts is of Portuguese descent.

Method:

1. Preheat oven.

2. In a mixing bowl, beat together butter and confectioner's sugar until creamy; stir in vanilla.

3. Add flour and salt, and beat mixture until smooth; stir in nuts.

4. Sprinkle a little confectioner's sugar on your hands and shape pieces of the mixture into ½" balls. Place on cookie sheets.

5. Bake until lightly browned. Remove from oven and quickly dip hot cookies in confectioner's sugar, being careful not to burn fingers.

6. Allow to cool, and roll again in confectioner's sugar.

Makes approximately 3 dozen.

INGREDIENTS:

½ cup butter (room temperature)
¼ cup confectioner's sugar
1 teaspoon vanilla essence
1 cup all purpose flour
⅛ teaspoon salt
1 cup finely chopped pecans, filberts, or walnuts.
Confectioner's sugar for rolling

Type of Pan:

Cookie sheets (ungreased)

Baking Temperature:

350°F

Baking Time:

15 minutes approximately, until lightly brown

Anecdote:

Hyacinth's baking day was Friday, and to make her cookies last all week she placed them in a cookie jar high on a kitchen shelf; far from her five children. As her policeman husband discovered one day, that didn't stop them from climbing up on each other's shoulders to steal them off the shelf.

INGREDIENTS:

½ cup margarine
½ cup sugar
1 egg (beaten)
½ teaspoon vanilla essence
1½ cups all purpose flour
½ teaspoon baking powder
½ teaspoon salt

Type of Pan:

Cookie sheet
(lightly greased)

Baking Temperature:

350°F

Baking Time:

Approximately 10 minutes

Alternative Ingredients:

Raisin cookies:
Add ½ cup raisins.
Lemon cookies: Omit vanilla;
add ½ teaspoon lemon
extract and 2 teaspoons
grated lemon rind.

Secret Touch:

No cookie cutter? Then Sarah
suggests the old-fashioned
way of using the rim of
a glass.

Anecdote:

Sarah says the good thing
about getting old, is eating as
many cookies as your
heart desires.

Sugar Cookies
by Sarah Bea Hayward

Sarah is a member of the Joy Club — a
seniors group run by the St. George's
Community Centre. Sandwiches, cakes,
and cookies are a regular feature of their
fall annual Fashion Show and Anniversary
Tea Party.

Method:

1. Preheat oven, lightly grease
   cookie sheet.

2. In a mixing bowl, cream margarine and
   sugar until light and fluffy.

3. Add beaten egg and vanilla with a
   teaspoon of flour to prevent
   mixture curdling.

4. Add flour, baking powder, and salt;
   mix well.

5. Divide into 4 portions and roll out each
   quarter on a lightly floured surface, until
   ⅛" thick.

6. Cut shapes with a cookie cutter and
   place on cookie sheets. Bake and then
   cool on rack.

Makes 20 cookies.

Cream Cheese and Tinned Shrimp Sandwiches

by Lillian Fountain

Lillian's husband came to Bermuda as British Airway's first manager. When Lillian was younger, she used to serve luncheon and tea parties in their ivy-trailing sun porch, and she did all the cooking herself from scratch.

Method:

1. Drain canned shrimp and sprinkle with lemon juice.

2. Spread cream cheese on each slice of bread.

3. Place shrimps on one side of bread and top with another slice.

4. Cut into fun shapes with cookie cutters.

INGREDIENTS:

Small can of shrimp
A little lemon juice
Small package of cream
cheese
White sliced bread

Secret Touch:

To avoid liquid from shrimps leaking, make sure cream cheese is spread evenly.

Anecdote:

Lillian says, when entertaining she always liked to be a little different. Cutting sandwiches in fun shapes with a cookie cutter is an unusual but attractive alternative.

The naming of teas is a difficult matter
It isn't just one of your everyday games-
Some might think you mad as a hatter
Should you tell them each goes by several names.
For starters each tea in this world must belong
to the families Black or Green or Oolong;
Then look more closely at these family trees-
Some include Indians along with Chinese.

The Naming of Cats
T.S. Eliot

INGREDIENTS:

1½ cups tepid water
1 cup milk
4 teaspoons margarine
3 teaspoons sugar plus ¾ cup
  sugar
2 teaspoons salt
1 teaspoon yellow food
  colouring (optional)
3 packages dried yeast
2 eggs
8 cups all purpose flour

Filling

1 cup shortening
2 teaspoons vanilla essence
1 package confectioner's
  sugar (1lb)

Type of Pan:

Cookie sheet (greased)

Baking Temperature:

325°F

Baking Time:

30 — 35 minutes

*Who remembers mead
now, or beef tea,
frumenty or other
native brews. Tea has
conquered them all.*

Libby Purves

Cream Puffs
by Joy Sticca

Joy has been indulging in these Cream Puffs since she was a little girl when her Aunt Effie and Aunt Ruth made them each year for Sunday school picnics. Joy is carrying on her family's summer tradition and now you too can share this winning recipe.

Method:

1. Divide water into 2 equal parts.

2. In a medium-sized pot, heat milk to boiling then turn off heat and add margarine, ¾ cup sugar, salt, ¾ cup water, food colouring.

3. When margarine and sugar have dissolved, set aside to cool in a large bowl.

4. In another bowl, add remaining ¾ cup water and 3 teaspoons of sugar. Sprinkle yeast on top. Set aside until yeast dissolves and bubbles.

5. In a separate bowl, beat eggs.

6. Add yeast mixture to cooled milk mixture and stir in eggs. Add at least 5 cups of flour, stir and knead in.

7. Add remaining flour and knead.

8. Place dough in a large greased bowl; allow to rise until double. Punch down dough and separate into rolls the size of golf balls.

9. Place on cookie sheets and leave to rise again until double.

10. Bake and then cool on rack. While rolls are baking, make filling.

Filling

1. In a mixer, cream 1 cup shortening and vanilla; add confectioner's sugar gradually.

2. Beat until fluffy.

3. When rolls are cool, cut down centre and add 1 teaspoon of filling.

Makes 30 — 40.

Secret Touch:

These can be frozen (if not all immediately gobbled up!).

Anecdote:

The word picnic comes from the French word piquenique. In the 1600s a picnic was a party where everyone contributed a dish of food.

Double Lemon Shortbread

by Ruth Harris

INGREDIENTS:

2 lemons
3 — 4 cups cake flour
1¼ cups confectioner's sugar
1½ cups butter
4 eggs
1 cup sugar
1 teaspoon baking powder

Type of Pan:

Two 8" round cake pans
(lightly greased)

Baking Temperature:

350°F

Baking Times:

1. 30 — 40 minutes
2. 30 — 35 minutes

Secret Touch:

Baking times are approximate — keep an eye on them to prevent browning too much. For perfect taste, always use butter never margarine.

Anecdote:

Shortbread is a traditional Scottish recipe. Ruth says Double Lemon Shortbread is a nice alternative.

Ruth has been very busy over the years as a Baptist Minister's wife. Many times she kindly hosted potluck luncheons and parties, and to this day still carries in her purse a little black book with her treasured recipes inside. Here is her mouth-watering recipe for shortbread with a twist — a twist of lemon!

Method:

1. Preheat oven, lightly grease pans.

2. Grate 1½ teaspoons lemon peel. Juice lemons and put aside.

3. In a mixing bowl, combine 3 cups flour with ¾ cup confectioner's sugar. Cut in butter with a pastry blender or knife. Knead together.

4. Divide mixture equally into 2 cake pans and pat into shape with hand. Bake 30-40 minutes. Cool for 20 minutes.

5. In a mixing bowl, beat eggs then add sugar, baking powder, ⅓ cup lemon juice, 1½ teaspoons lemon peel. Pour over cooked shortbread.

6. Bake for a further 30—35 minutes. Cool in pans for 5 minutes.

7. While cooling, mix ½ cup confectioner's sugar with 1 tablespoon lemon juice and drizzle over shortbread. Cut and store.

Each shortbread makes 12 slices.

Tomato Jam

by Kathleen Tatum

Kathleen was employed for many years as a cook at The Willowbank Hotel; a Christian retreat set in a picturesque palm-fringed bay in Somerset. She still lives there, making jams and jellies for afternoon tea and taking guests on walking tours. Here is her unusual recipe for Tomato Jam.

Method:

1. Scald tomatoes in boiling water and remove skins. Cut up into small pieces. Simmer in a pot until soft; turn off heat.

2. Divide tomato pulp into cup measures, and for each cup of pulp add 1 cup of sugar. Return mixture to pot.

3. Add lemon juice, rind, and ginger.

4. Boil until thick, stirring often to avoid burning.

5. Pour into warmed glass jars. Seal with wax, if you plan on storing.

INGREDIENTS:

1½ lbs. ripe tomatoes (about 6 medium)
Sugar
¼ cup lemon juice
1½ teaspoons lemon rind
1 tablespoon green ginger (chopped) or 1 teaspoon ginger powder

Type of Pan:

Large pot

Utensils:

Glass bottles with lids

Secret Touch:

To prevent the hot jam cracking the glass bottles, warm them gently in the oven set on very low, or rinse under hot tap water.

Anecdote:

Bermuda is a British Overseas Territory. Afternoon tea in Bermuda comes from the British tradition, when everyone stopped at four o'clock.

4

My Lords and Ladies

When banquets and other formal occasions begin their proceedings, it is not unusual for the Master of Ceremonies to announce: "My Lords and Ladies, may I present..."

This chapter presents recipes from some of Bermuda's life peers who have been knighted by HRH Queen Elizabeth II for services to the Country. Other special dignitaries have shared their favourites, and I have even included for humour a couple of other "Ladies of the Realm."

Hot Milk Cake 38

Pumpkin Loaf. 39

Banana Bread. 40

Raisin Bread. 41

Chocolate Brownies. 42

Coconut Shortbread. 43

Smoked Salmon Rollups 44

Chocolate Fruit Crisps 45

Coconut Macaroons. 46

Pecan Squares 47

Queen Athena's Dog Biscuits 48

INGREDIENTS:

1 cup milk
2 tablespoons butter
4 eggs
2 cups sugar
2 cups all purpose flour
2 teaspoons baking powder
½ teaspoon salt
2 teaspoons vanilla essence
2 tablespoons butter

Icing

½ cup confectioner's sugar
  (sifted)
1 teaspoon lemon essence
Water to mix

Type of Pan:

8" base funnel pan
(greased and floured)

Baking Temperature:

350°F

Baking Time:

40 — 50 minutes

Secret Touch:

You may halve ingredients
and bake in a loaf pan.

Hot Milk Cake
by Sir Richard Gorham

Sir Richard Gorham is a philanthropist and advisor to many individuals and charities. He was made Knight Bachelor in 1995, and also holds the DFC medal and CBE title. Lady Gorham referred me to Sir Richard's sister, Mrs. Wilkie, who has in her possession their mother's hand-written cookbook. She gave me this recipe for Hot Milk Cake.

Method:

1. Preheat oven, grease and flour pan.

2. In a pan, heat milk and butter until melted. Set aside.

3. In a mixing bowl, beat eggs until light and fluffy and leaves a trail. Add sugar.

4. In a separate bowl, mix together flour, baking powder and salt. Fold in egg/sugar mixture.

5. Add vanilla to milk mixture; stir into cake mixture.

6. Pour into funnel pan and bake. Cool on a rack.

Icing

1. In a small bowl, mix confectioner's sugar and lemon essence.

2. Add water, mix well and drizzle over cooled cake.

Pumpkin Loaf

by Lady Eileen Sharpe

Originally from Canada, Lady Sharpe met and married her late husband here in Bermuda. Sir John went on to become one of Bermuda's Premiers.

Lady Sharpe says this recipe for Pumpkin Loaf has been at the top of everyone's list for tennis and bridge parties; at Garden Club functions; luncheon meetings; Rose Club teas; and church fairs.

Method:

1. Preheat oven, grease and flour pan.

2. In a mixing bowl, beat eggs and sugar; add oil and pumpkin.

3. Sift dry ingredients; add to above. Stir in raisins.

4. Place in pan and bake.

Makes 1 loaf, which can be served buttered or plain.

INGREDIENTS:

2 eggs
1 cup white sugar
¾ cup oil
½ cup canned pumpkin
1½ cups all purpose flour
1 teaspoon baking powder
½ teaspoon cinnamon
1 teaspoon baking soda
½ teaspoon salt
1 cup raisins

Type of Pan:

Loaf pan
(greased and floured)

Baking Temperature:

350°F

Baking Time:

1 hour

Secret Touch:

This simple, quick recipe can be made ahead of time and tends to improve with age. It also freezes well.

There is a great deal of poetry and fine sentiment in a chest of tea.

—*Ralph Waldo Emmerson*

INGREDIENTS:

½ cup butter
1 cup sugar
2 eggs (beaten together)
1 cup mashed bananas
2 cups all purpose flour
1 teaspoon baking soda
½ teaspoon salt
1 teaspoon vanilla essence
¼ cup chopped walnuts
   (optional)

Type of Pan:

7½" x 3½" x 2½" Loaf pan
(greased and floured)

Baking Temperature:

325°F

Baking Time:

50 — 60 minutes

Alternative Ingredients:

During springtime, loquats
and Surinam cherries grow
wild in Bermuda. To turn this
recipe into loquat or Surinam
cherry bread: Replace baking
soda with three teaspoons
baking powder, and replace
bananas with loquats or
cherries (pitted and peeled).

Secret Touch:

For a crunchier taste, sprinkle
some chopped walnuts on
top (before cooking).

Banana Bread
by Lady Jacqueline Swan

Lady Swan is married to former Premier of
Bermuda, Sir John Swan. Originally from
Somerset, here in Bermuda, Lady Swan
started her career as a teacher and has
continued showing her love for children by
being involved in many children's
organisations. She shares with us one of
the Islands most traditional recipes — so
useful since many Bermudian gardens
grow bananas.

Method:

1. Preheat oven, grease and flour pan.

2. In a mixing bowl, cream butter and
   sugar until light and fluffy.

3. Add eggs then mashed bananas.

4. Add dry ingredients; stir in vanilla and
   walnuts.

5. Place in pan and bake.

6. Remove from oven and cool on rack.

We had a kettle; we let it leak;

Our repairing made it worse;

We haven't had any tea for a week;

The bottom is out of the Universe.

Rudyard Kipling (1865-1936)

Raisin Bread

by Lady Spurling

Lady Marion Spurling was born in the historic town of St. George's. Her husband was Speaker of the House, as was his father before him.

Lady Spurling took this simple, tasty recipe for Raisin Bread from an old family recipe book, hand-written in ink and still legible. It couldn't be easier.

Method:

1. Preheat oven, grease and flour pan.

2. In a bowl, mix together dry ingredients; add raisins.

3. Add milk and beaten egg; pour into pan and bake.

Makes 1 loaf.

INGREDIENTS:

2 cups all purpose flour
½ cup sugar
Pinch of salt
Raisins (about half a 15 oz. box)
2 teaspoons baking powder
1 cup milk
1 egg (beaten)

Type of Pan:

Loaf pan
(greased and floured)

Baking Temperature:

350°F

Baking Time:

45 minutes

Secret Touch:

Serve with butter, jam, and cream for a really delicious teatime treat.

Anecdote:

Lady Spurling remembers winter times, when, as a newly married woman, she would join her friends for afternoon tea. Gifts for charity were made during conversation over tea and cakes.

As for me and my house we will serve the Lord

INGREDIENTS:

1½ cups sugar
4 medium eggs
1 cup butter, unsalted
1 cup powdered cocoa
½ cup all purpose flour
8 oz plain chocolate
½ cup pecan nuts, chopped
½ cup white chocolate, cut
   into chunks, or ½ cup
   white chocolate chips

Type of Pan:

8" square pan
(lightly greased)

Baking Temperature:

350 — 375°F

Baking Time:

30 — 40 minutes

Secret Touch:

When cool, cut into wedges
or squares. For easier cutting
use a warm knife.

Chocolate Brownies
by Jennifer Masefield

Mrs. Masefield married Thorough Masefield, one of a long line of Governors to Bermuda since 1612.

Born in Uganda, this well-travelled couple has lived in Islamabad, Warsaw, and Kuala Lumpa. Their posting before Bermuda was back home in Lagos, Nigeria.

Here is her recipe for chunky, chocolate brownies.

Method:

1. Preheat oven. Lightly grease pan.

2. In a bowl, beat together sugar and eggs making sure sugar is fully dissolved.

3. Melt butter and whisk into eggs.

4. Sieve together cocoa and flour; add to egg mixture.

5. Melt plain chocolate in microwave, double boiler, or in a bowl over a pan of hot water; stir into mixture.

6. Add chopped nuts and white chocolate and turn into pan.

Bake.

Coconut Shortbread

by Sally Frith

Both St. George's and Hamilton have mayors. Sally's husband, William de Frith, became one of Hamilton's mayors. Sally and her friends learned the game of bridge from Bermuda bridge champion Marge Way. Meeting every Thursday for tea and bridge became a tradition and this recipe for Coconut Shortbread a favourite.

Method:

1. In a mixing bowl, cream together butter and sugars until fluffy.

2. Beat in eggs, 1 at a time.

3. Combine flour and coconut; stir into creamed mixture until soft dough.

4. Cover bowl with plastic wrap and refrigerate for at least an hour.

5. Preheat oven. On a floured surface, roll dough until ¼" thick. Cut dough into 3" rounds with a cookie cutter. Transfer onto an ungreased cookie sheet and bake until golden brown.

6. Cool on a wire rack.

Serves approximately 25.

INGREDIENTS:

1½ cups softened
   unsalted butter
½ cup brown sugar
¼ cup granulated sugar
2 eggs
2 cups cake flour
1 cup shredded coconut

Type of Pan:

Cookie sheet
(ungreased)

Baking Temperature:

350°F

Baking Time:

10 — 12 minutes

Secret Touch:

To keep fresh, store in an airtight container.

INGREDIENTS:

Two 3 oz. packages cream
  cheese
¼ teaspoon curry powder
10 — 12 oz. smoked salmon
  (finely chopped)
1 teaspoon fresh dill (finely
  chopped)
1 medium cucumber (peeled
  and finely chopped)
Pinch of ground pepper
2 tablespoons plain yoghurt
12 slices white sandwich
  bread

Secret Touch:

For a less expensive roll-up,
use drained tuna or canned
salmon.

Anecdote:

Did you know it was the
Americans who invented iced
tea and tea bags? (See History
of Tea chapter.)

Smoked Salmon Rollups

from the kitchen of the US Consulate

There are a number of Americans residing in Bermuda, including billionaire Ross Perot and his family. Maria DeSilva, one of the US Consulate's cooks, kindly shared this scrumptious recipe, which is served at private functions and parties.

Method:

1. In a mixing bowl, mix cream cheese with all ingredients except bread.

2. Remove crusts from bread. With a rolling pin, roll each slice to about ¼" thickness. Spoon salmon mixture across centre of each slice.

3. Bring sides of bread up over salmon mixture; secure with wooden toothpicks.

4. Place roll-ups seamside down, wrap in wax paper and cool in fridge for about 2 hours before serving.

5. Slice in wheels of ½" thickness and garnish with fresh dill sprigs.

Chocolate Fruit Crisps

by Gloria Prescott
Owner of motor yacht Lady Tamara

Over the years, Gloria and her husband, Nigel, have hosted many parties on board their yacht, named after their daughter, Tamara. Lady Tamara, or Lady T as she is affectionately known, has welcomed aboard royalty, television stars, singers and numerous wedding parties where they often serve these Chocolate Fruit Crisps.

Method:

1. Line an 8" square pan with greased paper, making sure to cover sides.

2. In a bowl, melt half the chocolate in a microwave or double boiler and spread evenly over paper.

3. In a pot, melt sugar and butter; stir in all the fruit and nuts. Heat for 2 minutes on stove.

4. Remove from heat; add Rice Krispies and liquor. Spread and press lightly over the chocolate in pan.

5. Melt remaining chocolate and use to cover mixture.

6. Chill and cut into fingers.

Makes about 24.

INGREDIENTS:

6 oz chocolate
¼ cup sugar
½ cup butter
1¼ cups chopped dates
⅓ cup chopped glazed cherries
⅓ cup chopped almonds
⅓ cup glazed pineapple and angelica
2 cups Rice Krispies
1 dessertspoon brandy or rum

Type of Pan:

8" square pan
(lined with greased paper)

Secret Touch:

In warm weather, store cookies in a covered container in the fridge. For a formal tea, each cookie may be placed individually in a paper cookie case.

INGREDIENTS:

4 egg whites
2 cups confectioner's sugar
1 teaspoon vanilla essence
½ cup all purpose flour
2 cups desiccated coconut

Type of Pan:

Greased cookie sheet or cookie sheet lined with rice paper

Baking Temperature:

325°F

Baking Time:

30 minutes

Alternative Ingredients:

For extra pizzazz, add a few drops of food colouring into the cookie mixture and decorate with halved glazed cherries on top.

Secret Touch:

Bake on high oven rack, as can brown before properly cooked through.

Anecdote:

A coconut is the biggest seed in the world and takes roughly three years to take root.

Coconut Macaroons

by Lady Astwood

Lady Astwood was born in Cuba, though she grew up in Jamaica. She met Sir James in Canada, and for many years prior to coming to Bermuda they lived together in Jamaica. In Bermuda, Lady Astwood is very involved with King Edward VII's Hospital Auxiliary.

This easy-to-make family recipe reminds her of swaying coconut palms.

Method:

1. Preheat oven.

2. In a mixing bowl, beat egg whites until stiff and form peaks.

3. Gradually add confectioner's sugar and vanilla, beating well after each addition.

4. Fold in flour and coconut.

5. Drop spoonfuls of mixture onto cookie sheet and bake until lightly brown.

Makes roughly 40 macaroons.

A woman is like a tea bag.

It's only when she's in hot water

that you realise how strong she is.

Address to U.S. Women's Congress (1981) —Nancy Reagan

Pecan Squares

by Lady Lolly Gibbons

Lady Gibbons' husband, Sir David Gibbons, is from an old Bermudian family. Sir David used to be a Premier as well as a Finance Minister.

Originally from Norway, Lady Gibbons loves to cook, but like the rest of us, just doesn't like the cleaning-up afterwards.

Method:

Crust

1. Preheat oven and grease pan.

2. Sift confectioner's sugar and flour into a mixing bowl. Cut in butter using 2 knives or a pastry blender, until fine and crumbly.

3. Pat crust into prepared pan and bake.

Topping

1. Mix melted butter, honey, cream and brown sugar together. Stir in pecans, coating them thoroughly.

2. After 20 minutes, remove crust from oven and spread on topping. Return pan to oven for a further 25 minutes.

3. Cool in pan before cutting into squares.

Makes roughly 48 squares.

INGREDIENTS:

Crust

⅔ cup confectioner's sugar
2 cups all purpose flour
1 cup butter or margarine

Topping

⅔ cup melted butter
½ cup honey
3 tablespoons cream
½ cup brown sugar
3½ cups pecans, chopped

Type of Pan:
9"x12" baking pan

Baking Temperature:
350°F

Baking Time:
Crust: 20 minutes
Topping: 25 minutes

Queen Athena's Dog Biscuits

by Anna Dawson

INGREDIENTS:

2 cups whole-wheat flour
¾ cup cornmeal
¼ cup Grapenuts cereal
1 teaspoon of garlic powder
½ teaspoon salt
2 tablespoons vegetable oil
¼ cup of molasses
2 eggs and ¼ cup of milk
　　mixed together

Type of Pan:

Cookie sheet
(ungreased)

Baking Temperature:

350°F

Baking Time:

20 — 30 minutes

Alternative Ingredients:

For added flavour, crumble chicken or beef bouillon cubes into dough.

Secret Touch:

For your dog's stocking treat at Christmas time, use festive shaped cookie cutters.

Anecdote:

"My mom's biscuits have milk bone beat," Queen Athena.

I couldn't resist including these dog biscuits when I found out the name of Anna's Whippet dog that lives on, aptly named, Jubilee Road.

Anna works at Endsmeet Animal Hospital in Devonshire and shares with us her recipe for the dog that reigns in your home!

Method:

1. Preheat oven.

2. In a mixing bowl, mix all dry ingredients together. Add oil, molasses, eggs and milk. Add more milk as needed to make a firm dough.

3. Lightly flour a rolling pin to prevent sticking and roll out dough until ½" thick.

4. Using cookie cutters, cut into shapes. Bake until lightly toasted.

Tea has intellectual, psychological and nutritional value. The physical act of getting up to put the kettle on stretches and unwinds muscles. A cup of tea is reassuring, especially in times of great pressure and stress.

Dr. David Lewis
Psychologist

5

Recipes from around the World

Many people of different nationalities live and work in Bermuda. This chapter highlights recipes from overseas residents fortunate enough to live on this beautiful Island.

Canada - Blueberry Scones 52

United States - Red Velvet Cake 53

Wales - Welsh Cakes 54

Scotland - Shortbread 55

Jamaica - Molasses Ginger Cookies . . 56

New Zealand - ANZAC Biscuits 57

South Africa - Crunchies 58

Ireland - Irish Soda Farl 59

Bahamas - Coconut Pound Cake . . . 60

Portugal - Malassadas
(Portuguese Donuts) 62

England - Sally Lunn Buns 64

INGREDIENTS:

2¼ cups all purpose flour
2 teaspoons baking powder
⅓ cup sugar
½ teaspoon salt
4 tablespoons butter
1 cup blueberries
1 egg
¾ cup milk
Egg for glaze

Type of Pan:

Cookie sheet
(lightly greased)

Baking Temperature:

350°F

Baking Time:

25 — 30 minutes

Secret Touch:

To prevent dough sticking, dip cutter into flour each time you cut out.

Anecdote:

Brenda suggests serving these scones freshly warm from the oven, when the blueberries are still soft. Spread with butter or jam and cream.

CANADA: Blueberry Scones
by Brenda Roberts

Some years ago, Brenda and Christopher Roberts fell in love with Bermuda during a summer vacation. They eventually moved here, and continue their love affair with the Island, living near the magnificent South Shore beaches — a romantic place, popular with the Roberts for sunset strolls.

Brenda's scone recipe, with fresh or frozen blueberries, is great for entertaining.

Method:

1. Preheat oven, lightly grease pan.

2. Put all dry ingredients into a mixing bowl.

3. With a pastry blender, or fingers, blend in butter until very fine crumbs. Add blueberries.

4. Beat egg with milk; add to dry ingredients. Mix until forms a ball.

5. Treating gently, roll out onto a floured surface until 1" thick.

6. Cut into circles with 2½" fluted pastry cutter. Place on cookie sheet and brush with egg wash.

7. Bake.

UNITED STATES: Red Velvet Cake

by Cami Ramsey

Cami and her husband, John, are Southern Baptist Missionaries — Bermuda being one of their assignments. Originally from Texas, Cami's family spent many years in Brazil, where John taught in a seminary. As well as an artist, Cami is an accomplished pianist and organist.

This elegant cake makes a welcome addition to any table.

Method:

1. Preheat oven, grease and flour pans.

2. In a mixer, beat eggs until fluffy. Add sugar and keep beating for about 4 minutes then add oil, vinegar, and food colouring.

3. In a separate bowl, mix dry ingredients.

4. Mix together milk and vanilla.

5. To original mixture in (2) above, add alternately, dry ingredients then milk and vanilla. Mix well.

6. Put into two layer pans and bake.

7. Ice with cream cheese icing or confectioner's sugar and milk.

INGREDIENTS:

2 eggs
1½ cups sugar
2 cups oil
1 teaspoon vinegar
1 bottle of red food colouring
2½ cups all purpose flour
1 teaspoon baking soda
1 teaspoon salt
2 tablespoons chocolate powder
1 cup buttermilk or milk with 1 teaspoon vinegar
1 teaspoon vanilla essence

Type of Pan:

Two x 8" layer cake pans (greased and floured)

Baking Temperature:

350°F

Baking Time:

30 — 35 minutes

Anecdote:

Cami recalls this recipe originally came from the Waldorf Astoria Hotel, where their red velvet carpet has welcomed guests from all over the world.

Tea urges tranquillity of the soul.

William Wordsworth Longfellow (1807-1882)

INGREDIENTS:

2 cups all purpose flour
2 teaspoons baking powder
Pinch of allspice or mixed
   spice
Pinch of salt
½ cup butter
½ cup sugar
¾ cup currants
1 egg (beaten)
Milk to mix

Type of Pan:

Griddle or frying pan

Cooking Temperature:

Low to medium

Cooking Time:

10 — 15 minutes

Secret Touch:

To test if cooked, cut one in half.

**Welcome is more
than two–thirds of
any feast.**

Old welsh saying

Croeso I Gymru!

(Welcome to Wales)

WALES:
Welsh Cakes
by Pat Jones

Pat has been visiting her family in Bermuda for 30 years, often twice a year. She always carries in her suitcase a box of Welsh Cakes for her son-in-law who loves them. In Wales, Welsh Cakes are always sold in baker's shops and at the markets, where they are cooked in front of you on griddles. Griddles are also known in Wales as "bakestones" (hence Welsh Cakes are locally known as Bakestones). This recipe has been handed down through many generations of Pat's family.

Method:

1. Sift flour, baking powder, spice and salt into a bowl. Rub in butter until resembles fine breadcrumbs; add sugar and currants.

2. Make a well in the mixture; add egg plus enough milk to make a soft dough.

3. Roll out, ½" thick, on a lightly floured surface. Cut out rounds with a 2½" pastry cutter.

4. Preheat a very lightly oiled griddle or frying pan; keep the heat low. Place cakes around the edges of pan, otherwise they burn easily. Turn occasionally and cook 10 — 15 minutes, until cooked through.

5. Cool on a rack and dust with sugar, if desired.

Makes about 18.

SCOTLAND: Shortbread

by Helen Stollery

Helen and her husband, Kevin, came to the Island for Kevin's secondment to the Bermuda Regiment. A highlight of Bermuda's summer season, is the regular Beating Retreat Ceremony performed by the Regiment Band in either St. George's or Hamilton.

This traditional biscuit comes from the kitchen of Helen's family, back in her Scottish homeland.

Method:

1. Preheat oven.

2. Mix flour and sugar in a mixing bowl.

3. Add butter; rub together with fingertips.

4. Scrunch mixture together to form a ball and turn out onto a surface. Knead until smooth (the warmth of your hands will make it smooth).

5. Pat or roll out to ½" thick and cut into fingers, 1" wide by 4" long.

6. Place on baking pan and prick tops all over with a fork.

7. Bake until a pale golden brown.

INGREDIENTS:

1½ cups all purpose flour
½ cup sugar
¾ cup butter

Type of Pan:

Baking pan
(ungreased)

Baking Temperature:

300 — 320°F

Baking Time:

20 — 30 minutes

Alternative:

Make into one large round cake, 5½" diameter and ¾" thick. Flute edges; prick all over with fork, mark into wedges with a knife or pizza cutter and bake.

Anecdote:

This melt-in-the-mouth Shortbread is called the traditional bridal cake of Scotland.

INGREDIENTS:

3 cups all purpose flour
2 teaspoons baking powder
1 teaspoon ground ginger
⅓ cup brown sugar
¼ teaspoon salt
1 cup margarine (softened)
5 oz. molasses

Type of Pan:

Cookie sheet
(ungreased)

Baking Temperature:

325°F

Baking Time:

8 minutes

Anecdote:

Ginger root, found at most supermarkets nowadays, is often grated and used as a medicinal tea. Ginger helps promote healthy joints.

Less neurotic than coffee, less sticky than juice, less problematic than alcohol, it goes well with real life: with cake, and sympathy, and moments of undemanding companionship.

Talking about Tea

Libby Purves

JAMAICA: Molasses Ginger Cookies
by Baltimore Walters

Chef Baltimore (Baltie) has worked at the Willowbank Hotel for many years. He and his wife, Dorret, are originally from Jamaica, where ginger is very much part of Jamaican cuisine, and can be found growing all over this Caribbean island. Baltie trained as a chef in Jamaica and later continued his training, here in Bermuda, at the Stonington Hotel College. His recipe for Molasses Ginger Cookies is typically Jamaican.

Method:

1. In a mixer, place dry ingredients with margarine. Mix until smooth.

2. Add molasses and mix until becomes dough (either using mixer or a wooden spoon).

3. Divide dough into 3 pieces and roll out each piece into a log, approximately 1½" wide x 8" long. Wrap each piece in wax paper; chill at least 1 hour.

4. Remove from fridge and preheat oven.

5. Slice logs and place on cookie sheet; flatten top with a fork and bake.

6. Cool on rack.

NEW ZEALAND: ANZAC Biscuits

by Cynthia Yeomans

Cynthia and her husband, Geoff, spend time between their homes in Bermuda and New Zealand. Each Christmas, both are involved in the annual children's pantomime performed at City Hall, staged by the Bermuda Musical and Dramatic Society (BMDS). A pantomime (originally from Britain) is a rowdy play, usually with a lively nursery rhyme theme such as Old Mother Goose. A man flamboyantly dressed as a woman usually performs the lead role.

Method:

1. Preheat oven, lightly grease pan.

2. In mixing bowl, combine flour, sugar, coconut and rolled oats.

3. In a pot, combine butter and syrup; stir over a gentle heat until butter has melted. Set aside.

4. Dissolve baking soda in boiling water, add to melted butter mixture and stir into bowl of dry ingredients.

5. To shape mixture, press into a small spoon, using a metal spatula to help; turn out these small mounds onto cookie sheets, allowing room for spreading.

6. Bake; remove from pan and cool.

Makes 30-40 (depending on spoon size).

INGREDIENTS:

1 cup all purpose flour
¾ cup sugar
1 cup desiccated coconut
1 cup rolled oats
½ cup butter
1 tablespoon golden syrup (or corn syrup)
½ teaspoon baking soda
½ teaspoon boiling water

Type of Pan:

Cookie tray
(lightly greased)

Baking Temperature:

350°F

Baking Time:

12 — 15 minutes

Anecdote:

In New Zealand, ANZAC Day commemorates the 1915 landing by 16,000 troops of the Australian and New Zealand Army Corps (ANZAC) on the Gallipoli Peninsula in Turkey, during World War I.

SOUTH AFRICA: Crunchies

by Thea Van Blerk

INGREDIENTS:

⅞ cup butter or margarine
2 tablespoons golden syrup
1 teaspoon baking soda
4 tablespoons milk
2 cups oats
1 cup desiccated coconut
1 cup sifted all purpose flour
1 cup sugar

Type of Pan:

11"x15" baking pan
(greased)

Baking Temperature:

375°F

Baking Time:

10 minutes

Secret Touch:

Don't press too hard into pan.

Anecdote:

Children love these healthy treats and often call them "toughies."

Bermudians are arguably some of the most travelled people in the world. Whether travelling overseas for education, work, shopping or vacations, the world is a Bermudian's oyster. While visiting my Bermudian friend, Sandy Frith-Brown, I met Russell Van Blerk who hails from South Africa. Like many Bermudians, Sandy has trained overseas, although not many people have been a medical student in Tasmania like him. Russell's uncle had been Sandy's Anatomy Professor and Thea, Russell's mother, was able to supply us with this family favourite for South African Crunchies.

Method:

1. In a pot, melt butter and syrup together.

2. Dissolve baking soda in milk; combine with butter and syrup. Add to dry ingredients (if mixture seems too dry add more milk).

3. Press onto baking pan and bake for 10 minutes. Switch off oven but leave in until golden brown. Cut into squares.

IRELAND:
Irish Soda Farl

by Ollie & Una McKittrick

As newly wed teachers, Ollie and Una came to Bermuda from their Irish homeland, where disputes in the early '60s forced them, as a mixed-faith couple, to look for a safe-haven. Bermuda provided the haven they were looking for to raise a family. Now retired, artistic Ollie paints, and Una is busy at the Visitors' Bureau in St. George's.

This recipe has been standard fare on Irish tables for centuries.

Method:

1. Preheat oven and lightly grease pan.

2. Mix dry ingredients and raisins in a bowl. Make a well in the centre and add enough buttermilk to make thick dough. Mixing should be done quickly, adding more milk if dough stiffens up.

3. Put dough onto a lightly floured surface. With floured hands, flatten into a circle 1½" — 2" thick.

4. Place on a baking pan. Usually a large cross is drawn on top (side to side), because after baking, Farl is divided into four. Bake.

INGREDIENTS:

6 cups all purpose flour
1 teaspoon baking soda
1 teaspoon salt
2 cups raisins
1 cup buttermilk

Type of Pan:

Baking pan
(lightly greased)

Baking Temperature:

350°F

Baking Time:

40 — 45 minutes
(test with skewer)

Alternative Ingredient:

If you don't have buttermilk, add vinegar or lemon juice to one cup of regular milk. Allow to stand for 25 — 30 minutes.

Secret Touch:

Wonderful served with fresh butter and strawberry or raspberry jam.

Anecdote:

Years ago, in many households throughout Ireland, Farl, along with potatoes, was a staple food; usually served at breakfast or tea-time.

INGREDIENTS:

1½ cups margarine
2¼ cups sugar
5 eggs
3 cups all purpose flour
3 teaspoons baking powder
¼ teaspoon salt
1 cup milk
1¼ cups coconut (flaked)

Icing

2 egg whites
1½ cups sugar
½ cup water
1 tablespoon light corn syrup
½ teaspoon vanilla essence
1¼ cups coconut (flaked)

Type of Pan:

10" cake pan
(greased and floured)

Baking Temperature:

325°F

Baking Time:

1 hour and 25 minutes

BAHAMAS: Coconut Pound Cake

by Constance Perry

Constance grew up on the small island of Spanish Wells in the Bahamas -- an island just 1½ miles long, where everyone knows everyone and each family has a coconut tree in their yard and a boat in the harbour. Constance was accustomed to picking her own coconuts for making a cake, until she met Bermudian, Eddie, who was visiting an Uncle on Spanish Wells. Within a year, he whisked her away to Bermuda, and to this day she occasionally dreams of picking fresh coconuts for baking cakes.

Constance's recipe has been slightly adapted for those of us who don't have a coconut tree in our own backyard!

Method:

1. In a mixing bowl, beat margarine and sugar together with an electric mixer until light.

2. Gradually add eggs one at a time, beating after each addition.

3. Combine flour, baking powder, and salt. Add to creamed mixture, alternating with milk. When blended, stir in coconut.

4. Pour batter into pan and bake.

5. Allow to cool in pan for 15 minutes. Remove and finish cooling on a wire rack.

7–Minute Icing

1. Combine egg whites, sugar, water and corn syrup in a medium pot.

2. Keeping heat low, beat mixture with an electric hand-mixer.

3. Beat until soft peaks form, about 7 — 10 minutes.

4. Remove from heat; beat in vanilla essence.

5. Spread icing over cooled cake; sprinkle with flaked coconut.

Secret Touch:

To prevent icing from burning, use a heavy-bottomed pot and keep heat very low.

Anecdote:

Spanish Wells is a tiny, fishing island whose population are descendants of American United Empire Loyalists. This quiet island has few tourists, only one resort hotel and one restaurant, although there are eight churches — one for every 50 inhabitants.

INGREDIENTS:

⅓ cup tepid water
1 teaspoon sugar
1 package yeast
5 eggs
⅓ cup sugar
1 teaspoon salt
5 ⅓ cups all purpose flour
⅓ cup margarine
½ shredded or grated lemon
    rind
⅓ cup lukewarm milk
Sugar for rolling cooked
    doughnuts

Type of Pan:

Deep fat frying pan

Cooking Temperature:

Medium/low

Cooking Time:

Roughly 4 minutes

*I did send for a cup of
tea, a China drink of
which I had never drunk
before.*

**Samuel Pepys Diary
(1666)**

PORTUGAL:
Malassadas
(Portuguese Donuts)
by Susanna Furtado

Susanna is a second generation Acorean, living here in Bermuda. Working for one of the many international insurance companies, her life is busy, but she still finds time to continue her learning with evening classes at the Bermuda College. Portuguese descendants living in Bermuda are known for their hard work and Susanna is no exception.

Among the Portuguese community, at any occasions, such as weddings or christenings, donuts are a must. Susanna learned to make these huge, flat donuts from her mother, Maria.

Method:

1. In a small bowl, dissolve yeast in water and sugar.

2. In a medium bowl, beat eggs with sugar and salt.

3. Into a large bowl, sift flour and rub in margarine. Sprinkle on and mix in grated lemon.

4. Make a well in centre of flour mixture; add yeast mixture, egg mixture, and lukewarm milk. Stir with a wooden spoon.

5. Use your hands to get mixture into a ball of dough; knead well.

6. Place in a lightly greased large bowl and allow to rise for about 3 — 4 hours.

Frying

1. Fill a deep fat frying pan 3/4 full with oil and heat until a small piece of bread dropped into fat turns golden brown (or the fat bubbles up round a wooden chopstick when dipped into).

2. Take pieces of the dough and cut into 2" squares, flour hands and gently pat squares down to flatten them a little. Drop into hot fat. Cook evenly on all sides.

3. Remove from oil with a draining spoon, drain on paper towel and roll in sugar. Cool.

Secret Touch:

If the donuts come out of the fryer with a doughy centre, turn down the heat, allowing them to cook longer.

INGREDIENTS:

2 ⅔ cups all purpose flour
Pinch of salt
2 eggs

Blend (A):
¼ cup butter
⅓ cup milk

Blend (B):
⅓ cup milk
1 teaspoon sugar
1 package yeast

Now for the tea of our host,

Now for the rollicking bun,

Now for the muffin and toast,

Now for the gay Sally Lunn.

Trial by Jury
Gilbert and Sullivan

ENGLAND:
Sally Lunn Buns

Courtesy of the Sally Lunn Museum

Sally Lunn (or Soli Luyon to give her her French name) was a Huguenot refugee, who, in 1680, went to work in a baker's shop in the ancient Roman and Saxon City of Bath, England. She introduced the baker to brioche-type breads and buns, and he became rich and famous. The original recipe — found in the 1930s in a secret cupboard over the shop's fireplace — is a closely guarded secret, and the Sally Lunn Museum and Tea Shop have kindly donated this alternative.

Method:

1. Sieve flour and salt into a mixing bowl.

2. Either in a bowl in the microwave, or pot on the stove, warm Blend (A) until the butter has just melted.

3. In a small bowl, mix Blend (B); allow to ferment for about 5 minutes.

4. Make a well in the flour and salt, pour in Blend (A) + (B). Add eggs.

5. Mix to a smooth dough and place in a greased bowl. Leave to rise in a warm place until double its size.

6. Turn dough onto a floured surface and knead lightly. Divide into 5 or 6 buns and, placing on a lightly greased cookie sheet; let rise again for about 30 — 40 minutes.

7. Bake. Remove from oven and cut buns into generous slices and serve (toasted if desired) with strawberry jam and clotted cream for a delicious, mouth-watering dream come true.

Type of Pan:

Cookie sheet
(lightly greased)

Baking Temperature:

450°F

Baking Time:

8 — 9 minutes

TEA TIME AT JASMINE,

A LUXURIOUS BERMUDIAN TRADITION. JOIN US.

THE *Fairmont*
SOUTHAMPTON PRINCESS

A Place in the heart.

South Shore 441-238-8000 www.fairmont.com

6

Afternoon Tea around the Island

Afternoon tea consists of quarter-cut sandwiches, an array of cakes, scones and, of course, a good pot of tea. Delightful teashops such as Penny Terceira's charming Victorian Tea-Rooms, serve an excellent traditional tea. The tradition of serving tea at 4 p.m. in Bermuda's hotels dates back to the 1920s. Originally only for guests of the hotel, upscale hotels such as Waterloo House and Southampton Princess now cater to non-guests, for a reasonable charge. How about an unusual location? You can charter a yacht, such as Nancy Dupperault's, Calabash, and sip tea as you cruise around the harbour. For this chapter, Bermuda's international, professional chefs have kindly shared some of their favourite recipes.

Lemon Cake - Waterloo House 68

Scones - Stonington Beach Hotel . . . 69

Mocha and White Chocolate Cake -
Newstead Hotel 70

Carrot Cake - Willowbank Hotel 72

Almond Croissants -
Pompano Beach Hotel 73

Toffee Breton - Calabash Cruising . . 74

Mini-baked White Chococolate
Cheesecakes -
Horizons and Cottages 76

Almond Cookies -
Grotto Bay Beach Hotel 77

Assorted Sandwiches -
Mrs. T's Victorian Tea-Room 78

INGREDIENTS:

Juice of 1 lemon
Zest of 2½ lemons
5 eggs
1½ cups sugar
2 cups all purpose flour
2 teaspoons baking powder
Pinch of salt
½ cup butter
½ cup double cream

Topping

Juice of 1 lemon
⅓ cup sugar

Type of Pan:

8"x3" deep round cake pan
(greased and floured)

Baking Temperature:

225°F

Baking Time:

2 — 3 hours

Lemon Cake
by Mark Lea
Waterloo House Hotel

After Mark's food technology training, he worked in various restaurants around Britain and, for a while, the P&O Cruise Lines employed him on their mini-cruises to Spain.

Since joining Waterloo House, Mark has specialised as a pastry chef. He makes this super moist Lemon Cake each day for afternoon tea.

Method:

1. Preheat oven, grease and flour pan and prepare lemons.

2. Whisk together eggs and sugar until very thick and creamy.

3. Stir in flour, baking powder, and salt. Add butter and lemon juice with lemon zest; stir in cream.

4. Place in cake pan and bake in middle of oven for 2 — 3 hours, or until cake tester comes out clean.

5. Take out of oven and prick holes in top with cake tester. Drizzle on the lemon sugar mix.

6. Allow to cool in pan.

Scones

by Frances Kelleher
Stonington Beach Hotel

Pastry chef and Londoner, Frances, learned her trade while working at the famous Savoy Hotel. Moving on, she worked for the Press Club and then the Knightsbridge store, Harrods. Harrods sent her to their first overseas store in Japan, where she trained Japanese chefs in the art of English afternoon tea!

Frances was en route to Australia when the Stonington Hotel manager happened to be in London and offered her a position in Bermuda.

Method:

1. Combine flour, sugar, and baking power in a mixing bowl.

2. Chop butter into small pieces and mix lightly until mixture resembles breadcrumbs.

3. Add egg and milk to the mix until combined — do not over mix.

4. Roll on a lightly floured surface, to about ½" thick.

5. Cut out rounds with a 1½" diameter, round cookie cutter.

6. Place on cookie sheet and bake.

INGREDIENTS:

1½ cups all purpose flour
2 tablespoons sugar
1 tablespoon baking power
¼ cup butter
1 egg
¼ — ⅓ cup milk

Type of Pan:

Cookie sheet (lightly greased)

Baking Temperature:

350°F

Baking Time:

15 — 20 minutes
(until golden brown)

Alternative Ingredients

For fruit scones, add 2 tablespoons of raisins. For cheese scones, add ½ cup of grated cheese. Scone mixture may be formed into one large round scone and divided into segments with a sharp knife (cut halfway through the dough).

Secret Touch:

The secret to a good scone is its consistency — make sure mixture is soft and work as quickly and lightly as possible.

Anecdote:

When she was in London, Amanda and a group of chefs would sometimes get together and swap recipes. This recipe came from the prestigious Connaught Hotel.

INGREDIENTS:

½ cup chocolate
¼ cup Espresso coffee
¾ cup butter
½ cup sugar
5 egg yolks
½ teaspoon vanilla essence
1⅛ cups all purpose flour
1¼ teaspoons baking powder
1¼ cups crème fraîche/sour
   cream
5 egg whites
¼ cup sugar (for meringue)

Filling

¼ cup white chocolate
1 cup fresh whipping cream

Glaze

½ cup butter
1 cup chocolate (dark)

Type of Pan:

8" deep cake pan
(lined and greased)

Baking Temperature:
Moderate Oven, 350°F

Baking Time:
40 minutes

Mocha & White Chocolate Cake
by Amanda Clark
Newstead Hotel

Amanda comes from Essex in England. She completed her chef's training at Westminster College, London. Since then, Amanda has worked as a pastry chef in hotels in Australia, the Isle of Man, and -- prior to the Newstead Hotel, Bermuda -- Euro Disney, Paris. Admitting to having a sweet tooth, Amanda shares this delicious cake made with real coffee.

Method:

1. Melt chocolate and add coffee.

2. In a mixing bowl, beat together butter and ½ cup sugar until light and fluffy.

3. Add egg yolks and vanilla to creamed mixture; stir in melted chocolate/coffee.

4. Mix baking powder into flour.

5. Alternatively add flour mixture with the crème fraîche/sour cream, folding mixture over with a metal spoon.

6. In a separate mixing bowl, beat egg whites until frothy and add ¼ cup sugar, a little at a time; continue beating until meringue forms. Fold gently into main mixture.

7. Place in pan and bake.

8. Cool on a rack.

Filling

1. Melt chocolate.

2. Whip cream until nearly stiff and mix in chocolate.

3. When cake is cooled, slice in half and fill with chocolate cream.

Glaze

1. Melt together butter and chocolate; pour over cake and chill.

Secret Touch:

Do not overheat the glaze.

INGREDIENTS:

4 egg yolks
1 cup sugar
1 cup carrots (grated finely)
1 cup almonds (grated finely)
1 lemon (juice and peel)
¾ cup all purpose flour
1 teaspoon baking powder
4 egg whites
½ teaspoon salt

Icing

2 cups confectioner's sugar
2 — 3 tablespoons lemon
   juice

Type of Pan:

9"x2" deep round cake pan
(lined, greased and floured)

Baking Temperature:

350°F

Baking Time:

50 minutes

Secret Touch:

After icing the cake, decorate
with small marzipan (almond
paste) carrots. Add green
food colouring for leaves and
orange for carrot shapes.

Carrot Cake
by Donald Duerr
Willowbank Hotel

Switzerland is known for its excellent
training in the hotel industry. Swiss born
Donald trained for three years in college
then went on to work in Swiss restaurants
like Aklin in Lug.

Coming to Bermuda, he worked at Ariel
Sands (which is part owned by the actor,
Michael Douglas), but eventually wound
up at Willowbank. He is now married to
Yvonne, who is a Bermudian.

This recipe is a light version of Carrot Cake
and comes from an area of Switzerland
called Aargau.

Method:

1. Preheat oven, line, grease, and flour
   cake pan.

2. In a mixing bowl, whip egg yolks and
   add sugar, a little at a time, beating until
   creamy.

3. Stir in carrots, almonds, lemon peel and
   juice.

4. Stir in flour and baking powder.

5. In a separate bowl, beat egg whites and
   salt until they form peaks; fold into rest
   of mixture.

6. Pour into cake pan and bake. Remove
   from oven, cool and ice.

Icing

1. Sift confectioner's sugar and stir in
   lemon juice.

Almond Croissants

by Jörg Rudolf
Pompano Beach Hotel

German born Jörg always liked to make sweets as a child, and when he left school he became an apprentice to a confectioner — as they call bakers of cakes and small sweets. After his three-year apprenticeship, he moved on to Brenners Park Hotel in the Black Forest, and then eventually to the Pompano Beach Hotel, Bermuda.

Method:

1. Preheat oven, lightly grease pan.

2. Put almond paste, sugar, salt, lemon juice and rind in mixing bowl.

3. Add 1 tablespoon of flour; mix until little nuts are formed.

4. Break in one egg at a time; continue mixing.

5. Put parchment or wax paper onto a tray with sliced almonds.

6. Using a small ice cream scoop (dipped in water) or a large tablespoon, scoop mounds onto wax paper.

7. Roll into sausage-shape logs 4" long, then curve into half moon croissant shapes (you may want to wear thin plastic gloves to prevent sticking).

8. Place on cookie sheet and bake, then cool on a cooling rack.

9. Melt chocolate in a double boiler or microwave and dip ends of croissants into chocolate. Let chocolate set.

INGREDIENTS:

1 lb. almond paste (raw marzipan)
1 cup sugar
Pinch of salt
½ a squeezed lemon and rind
1 tablespoon flour
2 eggs (grade A)
2 cups sliced almonds
16 oz bag chocolate chips

Type of Pan:

Large cookie sheet
(lightly greased)

Baking Temperature:

350°F

Baking Time:

9 minutes

Secret Touch:

Raw marzipan (almond paste) is essential for this recipe. The blocks we find in local supermarkets have too much sugar in. However, if that is the only thing available, then cut out the sugar from the recipe.

Anecdote:

Croissants do not originate from France but Vienna. To celebrate the end of the Turkish siege of the city, Vienna's pastry chefs invented the original pastry croissant: Pastries were shaped to replicate the crescent on a Turkish flag.

73

INGREDIENTS:

Toffee Filling

¼ cup butter
2 tablespoons honey
¾ cup light brown sugar
1 cup pecans (chopped coarsely)
1 cup walnuts (chopped coarsely)
½ cup almonds (chopped coarsely)

Cake

1 cup butter
1¼ cups sugar
5 egg yolks (large eggs)
1 teaspoon vanilla essence
1¾ cups all purpose flour

Egg Wash

1 egg yolk
1 teaspoon water

Type of Pan:

10" cake pan or 10" spring-form pan (greased and floured)

Baking Temperature:

350°F

Baking Time:

50 minutes (or till golden brown)

Toffee Breton

Nancy Dupperault
Calabash Cruising

When Nancy and her husband, Brian, lived in New York, she trained to become a pastry chef at the Peter Kump's New York Cooking School. Nancy puts her talents to use in Bermuda on board their newest venture – Calabash Cruising – where they offer catered cruises, including afternoon tea parties.

Toffee Breton is a classic French recipe from the northern Brittany region.

Method:

Toffee Filling

1. In a heavy pot, bring butter, honey, and sugar to a boil. Allow to boil for 3 minutes.

2. Stir in nuts; remove from heat and cool to room temperature.

Cake

1. Preheat oven, grease and flour pan.

2. In a mixing bowl, cream butter and sugar together. Continue beating while adding egg yolks, one at a time. Add vanilla; stir in flour.

3. Turn dough onto a well-floured surface (dough will be sticky). Divide dough in half; flour hands and press into cake pan.

4. Pour cooked toffee filling onto dough; spread and smooth to within ½" of sides of pan.

5. Flour hands again and press second half of dough onto top of toffee filling, to form top layer. Flour hands and make the top flat by lightly pressing dough - top should extend to sides of pan.

6. With the back of a fork, create a lattice design on top of cake. Brush with egg wash and bake in middle of oven. Cut into wedges size 1½" — 2".

Makes 10-12.

Alternative Ingredients:

Lemon zest can be substituted for vanilla (flour quantity should be decreased by 2 tablespoons).

Secret Touch:

This cake freezes well and can be made without the filling.

Anecdote:

Serving a "proper" tea on board a sailboat, at a 30-degree angle, can be an acrobatic experience. So, on board Calabash, flyaway goodies are kept to a minimum.

To Penny: inspired by a visit to her Tea Room, March 1997

A Cup of Tea

A female's such a simple soul,
Yet a creature so Profound,
She'd have the World be Paradise,
Where Love and Peace abound.
She knows the need of friendship,
And supports those of her Gender,
She knows the art of Listening,
When, just a Nod can be so tender.
A Cup of Tea—a biscuit,
Is all that it does take,
To put the World in place again,
Or perhaps! A piece of Chocolate Cake!
For Females understand each other,
And no subject is too small,
For earnest consultation, when
The heart needs Overhaul.
I spent the day with Mary,
And know not years or miles can end,
That special bond of Sisterhood,
That comes - from being Friends

Barbara Ruth Neish
Paget, Bermuda

INGREDIENTS:

Pre-baked pastry cases
6 oz. white chocolate
1½ oz. double cream
8 oz. package cream cheese
   (softened)
⅓ cup sugar
¼ teaspoon salt
2 eggs (beaten)
½ teaspoon vanilla essence

Type of Pan:

Tartlet pan
(tartlet papers optional)

Baking Temperature:

325°F for 15 minutes,
then 225°F

Baking Time:

15 + 10 minutes

Alternative Ingredients:

Add a little Bailey's Irish
Cream to the finished
mixture.

Secret Touch:

Best served same day.

Anecdote:

Relais & Chateaux hotels and
restaurants must comply with
their "five C's" motto —
character, courtesy, calm,
charm, and cuisine.

Mini-baked White Chocolate Cheesecakes

by Susan McCann
Horizons & Cottages

Susan is a chef at the Horizons, a charming cottage colony resort, not far from Bermuda's South Shore beaches. After attending catering college, Susan went straight to the Isle of Man, a green and pleasant island in the Irish Sea, famous for Manx Cats (cats with no tails).

The big city of London beckoned, so she moved to the prestigious Savoy Hotel. Later on, she specialised as a patisserie at the Lucknam Park Hotel, Leamington Spa, which, like Horizons, is a member of the Relais & Chateaux group of hotels.

Method:

1. Preheat oven.

2. Put pre-baked pastry cases into tartlet pans.

3. Melt chocolate in a bowl over hot water or double boiler; add cream.

4. In a separate bowl, with an electric mixer, whip cream cheese, sugar, and salt.

5. Slowly add beaten eggs and vanilla essence; pour in the chocolate mixture.

6. Spoon mixture into tartlet cases. Bake slowly: 325°F for 15 minutes, turn oven down to 225°F and finish baking. When baked through, the filling will pop back up with a light touch of a finger.

Makes 36 small tartlets.

Almond Cookies

by Koeswana Sumirat
Grotto Bay Beach Hotel

Koeswana is one of many chefs in Bermuda from the Far East -- Indonesia being his native land, where he trained as a pastry chef. Koeswana tells us "speculas," or mixed spices, are typically used in Far Eastern countries, where they are part of the everyday culinary experience. These unusual Almond Cookies are both crisp and spicy.

Method:

1. Preheat oven, lightly grease cookie sheet.

2. Put water, brown sugar, and butter into a pot and bring to boil; cool to lukewarm.

3. Put the egg yolks into a large bowl. When the sugar and butter mixture has cooled, mix in egg yolks and add almonds, flour, cinnamon, cloves and vanilla. Mix to a dough.

4. Roll into log shapes and slice ⅜" thick; place on a cookie sheet and bake.

INGREDIENTS:

8 tablespoons water
2 cups brown sugar
¾ cup butter
6 egg yolks
2½ cups sliced and
   chopped almonds
¾ cup all purpose flour
1 tablespoon cinnamon
1 teaspoon ground cloves
1 teaspoon vanilla
   essence

Type of Pan:

Cookie sheet
(lightly greased)

Baking Temperature:

400°F

Baking Time:

15 — 20 minutes

There are few hours in life more agreeable than the hour dedicated to the ceremony of afternoon tea.
Henry James

SANDWICH IDEAS

Cashews and chicken

Cucumber with dill

Cream cheese
and diced nuts

Egg salad with
a pinch of curry

Cream cheese and
a little blue cheese mixed

Tuna salad

Roast beef and mustard

Turkey

Cream cheese and shrimp

Stilton, walnut and
thinly sliced pear

*Tea is the
ultimate form
of hospitality.*

**Amy
Vanderbilt**

Assorted Sandwiches

*by Penny Terceira
Mrs. Tea's Victorian Tea-Room*

Penny's love for tea and tea memorabilia led her to become a collector, so much so that she longed to open her own tea-rooms. Set in a small cottage near Port Royal Golf Club, her tea-rooms have become a favourite of locals and visitors alike. Each room is decorated in a theme, such as the Royal Room, and each one is full of interesting knick-knacks and antiques.

Named after the Earl of Sandwich, sandwiches are a vital part of any proper tea party. When served for afternoon tea, sandwiches are small and delicate, often cut in a variety of shapes; just the way Penny makes them. Her tea-rooms serve a tea-for-two, which consists of 12 finger sandwiches, 10 little sweets such as lemon curd tartlets, date squares, lemon shortbread, brownies and, of course, a scone with clotted cream and jam. Here, Penny gives some examples of her sandwiches. As well as these, she serves chicken, egg salad and turkey sandwiches with romaine lettuce as filler.

After cutting off the crusts, the sandwiches are cut into quarters, oblongs, rounds, or other shapes using cookie cutters. Unless otherwise stated, you may use brown or white bread.

Tuna with Chopped Walnuts:

Using your own favourite tuna mixture, sprinkle chopped nuts on top. If you mix the nuts in too early, prior to serving, they will become moist.

Cheese:

Shred Cheddar and Swiss cheese together; mix with some mayonnaise and a drop of hot sauce.

Minced Ham:

Mince the ham and mix in green relish, to required taste. Add some mayonnaise to hold the mixture together and for spreading.

Cucumber:

Cut rind off cucumber and slice thinly. Spread white bread with a thin layer of cream cheese and place cucumber on. Cut into quarters. Place two quarters on top of each other and tie with narrow ribbon into a parcel.

Asparagus:

Lightly spread the bread with mayonnaise. Using one long stalk, roll bread around asparagus. Cut sandwich into 2 halves. You may use canned asparagus.

Crunchy Peanut Butter:

Spread bread with peanut butter and top with some "Fluffy" marshmallow sauce. Lettuce could be added if wished.

Open-faced Smoked Salmon:

Spread bread with cream cheese, place salmon on top and decorate with a slice of onion and capers.

Breads

White
Brown
Whole Grain
Nut Breads
Raisin Bread
Cinnamon Swirl

Crispings

Lettuce
Watercress
Mustard and Cress
Alfalfa Sprouts
Thinly Sliced Peppers

Additions

Mustard
Honey Mustard
Dijon Mustard
Sweet Pickle
Chutney

"I can just imagine myself sitting down at the head of the table and pouring tea", said Anne, shutting her eyes ecstatically, "and asking Diana if she takes sugar! I know she doesn't but of course I'll ask her just as if I didn't know."

Anne of Green Gables
L.M. Montgomery

7

Best of British

Teatime, along with other colonial customs, is part of Bermuda's special British heritage. When Britain laid claim to this dependent territory in the early 1600s, tea was not one of the supplies brought with the first settlers. After tea became popular in Britain, so it did in Bermuda, and in this chapter you'll find some British favourites that have crossed the waters.

Victoria Sandwich. 82

English Sponge Cake 83

Swiss Roll. 84

Bakewell Tarts 86

Auntie Joan's Iced Slices 88

Chocolate Eclairs 90

Christmas Mince Pies 91

INGREDIENTS:

¾ cup butter or margarine
¾ cup sugar
3 large eggs (beaten)
1½ cups all purpose flour
1½ teaspoons baking powder
Jam
Confectioner's sugar

Type of Pan:

Two 7" cake pans
(greased and floured)

Baking Temperature:

350°F

Baking Time:

20 — 30 minutes

Secret Touch:

To prevent the cooling rack indenting top of cake, place a folded tea cloth on palm of one hand and turn cake onto it. Turn cake topside up with cloth underneath before placing on rack.

Anecdote:

This cake is said to have been popular with Queen Victoria, hence the name.

Victoria Sandwich
by Ann Coakley

Ann is a trained food and nutrition teacher, having taught in Bermuda for quite a few years. Originally from Salisbury, England, Ann shares this basic recipe from the teaching file she always keeps handy — a firm favourite for any curriculum or tea book.

Method:

1. Grease and flour 2 cake pans (layer/sandwich pans) and preheat oven.

2. In a mixing bowl, cream (beat) margarine until soft. Gradually add sugar, beating until mixture is light and fluffy.

3. Beat in eggs, a little at a time (add a little flour if mixture starts to curdle).

4. With a large metal spoon, fold in flour and baking powder.

5. Divide mixture between the 2 pans and bake.

6. After baking, allow to cool for 1 — 2 minutes in tins then turn out onto a cooling rack.

7. When cool, fill with jam and dust top with confectioner's sugar.

Throughout the whole of England the drinking of tea is general. You have it twice a day though the expense is considerable, the humblest peasant has his tea like a rich man.
La Rochefoucauld (1784)

English Sponge Cake

by Sally Frith

Sally originates from Kent in England, where her mother used to serve this old-time British sponge cake to friends as a light accompaniment to Bridge afternoon teas.

Method:

1. Preheat oven. Grease and flour cake pans.

2. Whisk eggs in an electric mixer at top speed for 5 minutes. Add sugar and continue whisking at top speed for 15 minutes.

3. Mix together baking powder with flour; add to whisked mixture a little at a time, folding in with a large metal spoon.

4. Pour into 2 cake pans and bake on middle shelf.

5. Remove from oven and allow cakes to cool slightly before removing from pans. Turn out gently as they are liable to break. Cool on a cooling rack.

6. When cakes are cool, turn one cake over and spread the other with jam and cream. Place together.

INGREDIENTS:

3 eggs
½ cup sugar
¾ cup all purpose flour
1½ teaspoons baking powder

Filling

Raspberry jam and freshly whipped cream

Type of Pan:

Two 7" or 8" cake pans (greased and floured)

Baking Temperature:

350°F

Baking Time:

25 minutes

Secret Touch:

For the perfect taste, do not skimp on jam or cream. Confectioner's sugar may be dredged on top of finished cake.

INGREDIENTS:

3 eggs
1 cup sugar
½ teaspoon vanilla essence
   (optional)
1 cup all purpose flour
¼ teaspoon salt
½ teaspoon baking powder
2 tablespoons tepid water

Filling and Rolling

3 — 4 tablespoons warmed
   jam
Extra sugar for rolling

Type of Pan:

8"x12" jellyroll pan
(lined and greased)

Baking Temperature:

375°F

Baking Time:

12 — 15 minutes

Swiss Roll
by Alice W. Wilson

In 1942, Alice Wilson was headmistress of the old Bermuda Domestic Science School, and compiled a cookery textbook called A Junior Cookery Book. In the foreword, Jessie C. Hollis Hallett, Chairperson, writes, "It [this book] is not intended to take the place of many splendid cookery books already published, but merely to help children to learn the simple rules of cookery, and so aid them to put their lessons into practice in their homes." It is up to you to decide whether this ideal is still in practice in schools today.

Miss Wilson's recipe for Swiss Roll is as good today as it was in 1942.

Method:

1. Line and grease a jellyroll pan. Preheat oven.

2. In a mixing bowl, beat eggs; add sugar and continue beating until mixture is thick and creamy. Mixture should leave a thick trail on top. Add vanilla if desired.

3. Fold in half the flour, salt, and baking powder.

4. Add 2 tablespoons of tepid water then add remaining flour, salt, and baking powder. Fold in gently -- do not over stir.

5. Pour into prepared pan, smoothing out the corners. Bake in top ⅓ of oven.

6. Meanwhile, warm jam in double boiler or microwave. Prepare a sheet of waxed or greased paper with sugar sprinkled on it.

7. When baked, turn cake immediately lengthways onto sugared paper.

8. Remove cooking paper and cut off long edges of cake, (which are too tough for rolling).

9. Spread with jam.

10. To enable rolling, make a cut ½" from short edge nearest to you. Using the sugared paper, roll up cake; start by tucking in at the cut edge. Keep rolled in the paper and cool on a wire rack; remove paper when cool.

There are few more agreeable moments in life than tea in an English country house in winter. It is dark at 4 o'clock. The family and guests come in from the cold air. The curtains are drawn, the open wood fire is blazing, the people sit down around the table and with a delightful meal — for the most attractive food in England is served at afternoon tea-drink of the cheering beverage.

William Lyon Phelps (1930)

INGREDIENTS:

Pastry

2 cups all purpose flour
⅓ cup margarine
⅓ cup lard
Water to mix (approximately
    6 — 8 tablespoons)

Filling

¼ cup butter
¼ cup sugar
1 egg
1¼ cups ground almonds
1 cup cake crumbs
2 teaspoons almond essence
Raspberry jam

Topping

Confectioner's sugar

Type of Pan:

Tartlet pans

Baking Temperature:

400°F

Baking Time:

25 — 30 minutes

Bakewell Tarts

by the author — Mair Harris

In any town in Britain you will find a baker's shop window full of tempting teatime fare. Many bakers' shops have a teashop inside, so you can taste your favourite pastry on the spot with a 'nice cup of tea.'

Among the scones, Eccles cakes, Chelsea buns and crumpets, you will likely find these traditional tarts, which can be served warm or cold.

Method:

1. Make pastry as per the shortcrust pastry method (see next recipe for Iced Slices).

2. Roll pastry out into a circle and chill in fridge.

3. In a mixing bowl, cream together butter and sugar until thick and white.

4. Beat in egg; add ground almonds, cake crumbs and almond essence.

5. Remove pastry from fridge and cut out circles with a pastry cutter, to fit tartlet pans.

A small tray of tea things was arranged on the table, a plate of hot buttered toast was gently simmering before the fire.

Pickwick Papers, Charles Dickens

6. Put about ½ teaspoon of raspberry jam in each tart and spread creamed mixture on top. Bake.

7. For decoration, sift confectioner's sugar on baked tarts.

Alternative Ingredients:

Lemon curd or apricot jam instead of raspberry jam. As a change from the tarts, create a pie.

Anecdote:

There is an actual town called Bakewell in Derbyshire, England. The old Bakewell Pudding Shop, in this rural Peak District town, still makes the original 1860 recipe.

INGREDIENTS:

Pastry

3 cups all purpose flour
1 teaspoon baking powder
6 tablespoons butter
6 tablespoons lard
Water to mix

Custard

8 tablespoons custard
   powder
2 cups milk
3 tablespoons sugar

Icing

2 cups confectioner's sugar
Water to mix (about 1 — 2
   tablespoons)

Next to water, tea is the English man's proper element. All classes consume it, and if you are out on one of London's streets early in the morning, one may see in many places small tables set up under the open sky, round which coal-carters and workmen empty their cups of their delicious beverage.

Erik Geijer (1809)

Auntie Joan's Iced Slices
by Joan Smith

My Auntie Joan has made iced slices for as long as I can remember. They are a firm favourite at cricket teas when the players come off the field at change of play.

Cricket is, of course, very much a British and Commonwealth game, and was introduced into Bermuda in the 1800s. Bermuda's annual Cup Match cricket game is a two-day holiday to commemorate the abolition of slavery in 1834.

Method:

Pastry

1. Place flour, baking powder, butter and lard into a bowl. Rub in, until resembles fine breadcrumbs.

2. Add water and mix by hand until mixture comes away from the sides of the bowl in a ball.

3. Knead lightly.

4. Cut pastry in half; roll out each piece into a rectangle.

5. Place one rectangle in a pastry pan ensuring it covers the bottom and sides.

Custard

1. Using the ingredient measurements in this recipe, follow directions on Bird's custard can for making custard.

2. Pour custard onto uncooked pastry and top with remaining pastry.

3. Bake.

4. Cool in pan.

Icing

1. Sift confectioner's sugar into a bowl and add water, a little at a time.

2. Ice the pastry top.

3. When icing is set, cut into bars.

Type of Pan:
Pastry pan

Baking Temperature:
400°F

Baking Time:
30 — 35 minutes

INGREDIENTS:

½ cup water
¼ cup margarine or butter
⅔ cup all purpose flour
Pinch of salt
2 eggs (beaten)
Melted chocolate
Whipped cream

Type of Pan:

Cookie sheet
(greased)

Baking Temperature:

400°F

Baking Time:

15 minutes

Alternative Ingredients:

Instead of eclairs, choux pastry may be made into profiteroles. Onto a cookie sheet, spoon the mixture (about the size of golf balls). Use thick lemon pie filling or thick custard instead of cream. Smother in chocolate.

Chocolate Eclairs
by the author — Mair Harris

Choux pastry is not something often made these days, but it's really quite simple. Filling piping bags and washing them afterwards may seem time consuming, but the end result for teatime, or as a dessert, is certainly worthwhile. For extra convenience buy throwaway piping bags.

Method:

1. Put water and margarine in a pot and heat. Ensure margarine is fully melted, and with a wooden spoon, beat in flour and salt.

2. Allowing mixture to cool slightly, beat in eggs gradually to form a stiff consistency for piping. Dough should be just soft enough to pipe.

3. Fit a piping bag with a large plain nozzle. Fill bag and pipe eclairs about 2" — 3" long (resembles small cigars) onto cookie sheet.

4. Bake until crisp and lightly brown.

5. Remove from oven (turn oven off); using a knife, split lengthways (like a hotdog roll), leaving attached on one long side.

6. Scoop out any uncooked dough and return to oven for 2 minutes to dry out.

7. Cool on a rack, then dip tops into melted chocolate and fill with whipped cream.

Christmas Mince Pies

by the author — Mair Harris

There's nothing like a traditional British Christmas at home, where, after the lunchtime turkey, rich plum pudding is served for dessert. Later on, if anyone can face eating again, Christmas cake, chocolate log and mince pies are served for afternoon tea. Christmas cake is dark and heavy with dried fruit often steeped in brandy before cooking. The cake is then covered with marzipan (almond paste) and white royal icing, fluffed up to look like snow.

The chocolate log is a Swiss roll with chocolate or cocoa added to the recipe; filled with cream then iced with chocolate icing to resemble a log of wood. Often, an artificial robin or sprigs of holly are set on top for decoration. Mince pies are usually available in baker's shops before Christmas. For good luck, the saying goes, "You should eat 12, one for every month of the year — each one must be prepared by a different cook!"

Method:

1. Roll out pastry about ⅛" thick.

2. Cut out half into rounds to fit tartlet pans.

3. Cut remaining pastry into rounds to serve as tops.

4. Fill pies with mincemeat. Brush edge of pastry with water and put on lids. Press edges of pastry together.

5. Brush pastry tops with egg and make a small cut in top to let out steam.

6. Bake.

7. When cool sprinkle tops with confectioner's sugar.

INGREDIENTS:

Make your favourite pastry
Mincemeat
Egg for brushing pastry
Confectioner's sugar

Type of Pan:

Tartlet pans

Baking Temperature:

400°F

Baking Time:

25 — 30 minutes

Alternative Ingredients:

For added sweetness, confectioner's sugar and water can be used to ice the top of pies. To give the pies some kick, add a drop of Bermuda Rum or Rum Essence to the mincemeat. Instead of sealing pies with pastry tops, cut pastry star shapes and place on top of mincemeat.

VICTORIA SPONGE CAKE
by Joyce Zuill

½ cup of butter
½ cup sugar
2 large eggs
1 cup flour
1 teaspoon baking powder

Method

Sift the flour and baking powder. Heat oven to 350 – 375°F. Cream butter and sugar until soft and light. Beat in the eggs. Fold in the flour and baking powder with a spoon.

Divide the mixture between two 7-inch greased and floured sandwich cake pans.

Bake for 15 – 20 minutes until firm to the touch. (Test with a skewer—it should come out clean).

Cool for a few minutes and then turn *CAREFULLY* out of the pans.

To Serve

Fill between the layers with jam or whipped cream. Top with sifted icing sugar.

Add a few drops of lemon or orange essence to the mixture if wished.

8

High Tea

In the 19th century, high tea came about as a meal for the working family. Lunch (called dinner just to confuse) was the main meal of the day. With illumination only from candles, a meal was needed for the family before dark, so high tea became a family meal eaten between 5 and 7 p.m. (This custom of high tea can still be found in many parts of Britain, with the name shortened to tea). A traditional high tea includes savoury and sweet foods, with the savoury eaten first. Savoury items may be cold cuts; pies and pasties (served either hot or cold); and a salad. Bread and butter, cheese and jam are also on the table. The sweets that follow will be cakes, cookies and fruit pies, and, if company is present, Jell-O and fruit salad are likely additions. And, of course, pots of good strong tea are always an accompaniment.

Sausage Rolls 94

Scotch Eggs 95

Cheese Triangles 96

Shepherd's Pie 97

Pikelets. 98

Cornish Pasties 99

Welsh Rarebit 100

Cod Fish Cakes 101

Banana Chutney. 102

Pickled Onions. 103

Loquat Upside-Down Cake. 104

INGREDIENTS:

Pastry

2 cups all purpose flour
Pinch of salt
½ cup Crisco
8 — 12 tablespoons cold
   water

Filling

½ lb. sausage meat or 4
   sausages

Glaze

Egg wash

Type of Pan:

Baking pan with ½" sides

Baking Temperature:

400°F

Baking Time:

20 — 30 minutes

Alternative Ingredient:

For extra flavour, mixed
herbs may be added to
sausage meat.

Secret Touch:

To prevent greasy rolls,
remove quickly from pan.

Sausage Rolls
by Judy Ratteray

Judy is a Bermudian who has taught home economics in Bermuda schools for over 30 years and is currently a family studies teacher. Judy and I started our teaching careers together, working in the same Home Economics Department in St. George.

You can be assured this recipe for Sausage Rolls is tried and true.

Method:

1. Preheat oven. Sift flour and salt into a mixing bowl.

2. Cut Crisco into small pieces and rub into flour until mixture resembles fine breadcrumbs.

3. Add water, 1 tablespoon at a time, stirring with a spatula. Using one hand, collect together to make a firm dough; knead lightly.

4. Roll pastry into an oblong. Cut this in half, lengthways.

5. Divide sausage meat into 2 pieces, dust with flour then roll out to fit the pastry strips.

6. Lay sausage meat on top of pastry strip. Wet edge of each strip and fold other side over meat; press pastry edges together and seal.

7. Brush with egg wash, and then with a sharp knife, make small diagonal cuts along top of pastry. Cut into small or big rolls, as desired. Bake until pastry is golden brown.

Scotch Eggs

by Susann Richardson

Susann spent her early years in Ipswich in the East of England, but has lived in Bermuda for over 30 years. Spending some of her career as supervisor of the Catering Department of the Bermuda Telephone Company, Susann is in an environment she enjoys. In her spare time she has two main loves: entertaining and adventure travel.

This tasty and filling Scotch Egg recipe is a very traditional one, often served at picnics and high tea.

Method:

1. Peel hard-boiled eggs and pat dry with towel.

2. In a bowl, mix sausage meat, salt, pepper and herbs.

3. Divide into 6 portions. Taking one portion, pat out sausage meat on your hand or on a lightly floured surface. Press sausage meat around hard-boiled egg, leaving no gaps.

4. Pass through flour, then dip in beaten egg and roll in seasoned breadcrumbs. Repeat until all eggs are covered.

5. Deep fat fry for 10 minutes, or shallow fry on all sides.

6. Drain on paper towel; cool. Cut in half lengthways and serve.

INGREDIENTS:

6 hard-boiled eggs
Roughly 1¼ lbs. sausage meat or skinned sausages
1 teaspoon salt
½ teaspoon pepper
1 teaspoon mixed herbs
Flour on a plate
1 beaten egg and dash of hot sauce
2 cups breadcrumbs

Type of Pan:

Deep fat fryer or frying pan

Cooking Time:

10 minutes

Secret Touch:

For crispier eggs: repeat dipping in egg and then breadcrumb mixture. For less fat, try baking in oven at about 350°F for 15 minutes.

INGREDIENTS:

1 cup butter or margarine
1 cup sour cream
2½ cups all purpose flour
2 cups strong cheddar cheese
(grated)

Type of Pan:

Cookie sheet
(greased)

Baking Temperature:

350°F

Baking Time:

35 minutes

Anecdote:

Catherine is author of the
Maverick Guide to Bermuda
(Pelican Books) -- published
spring 2000 -- a fully
comprehensive guidebook,
which includes all the Island's
favourite tea spots.

Cheese Triangles
by Catherine Harriott

Before coming to Bermuda, British born
Catherine and her husband, Tony, worked
in Jersey in the Channel Islands, and also
lived for eight years in Canada. It was after
a day of cross-country skiing in the
Okanagan Valley, British Columbia, that
Catherine first tasted these Cheese
Triangles.

Method:

1. Mix first three ingredients together in a
   bowl. Knead into a firm ball and
   refrigerate for at least a half-hour.

2. Preheat oven and grease cookie sheet.
   Divide into small pieces then roll into
   thin oblongs. Cut into squares about
   4"x4".

3. Spread ½" thick layer of cheese onto
   each square. Damp edges with water;
   seal and pinch into a triangle shape.

4. Bake until golden brown. Serve warm or
   cold.

Shepherd's Pie

by the author — Mair Harris

Many years ago, the Bermuda School of Home Economics produced a cookery book for use in island schools. Like its predecessor, A Junior Cookbook, many of the recipes are good old standards that stand the test of time. The cultural mix of teachers of that era is revealed -- with recipes such as gingerbread from Bermuda; brownies from North America; kedgeree from Britain; curried mutton from the West Indies.

Today, many mothers and grandmothers recall this red cookbook, which was part of each girl's home economics' curriculum. Here's one of the recipes for Shepherd's Pie.

Method:

1. Heat oven and grease ovenproof dish.

2. In a frying pan, fry onion with fat; add flour, then stock. Heat for 5 minutes.

3. Add meat, herbs, and seasonings, and simmer until cooked through.

4. In a bowl, mash potatoes, add milk and seasoning; mix well.

5. Put meat into dish and cover with mashed potatoes. Using the back of a fork, rake lines along top. Bake until golden brown on top.

INGREDIENTS:

1 chopped onion
2 tablespoons fat
3 tablespoons all purpose flour
¾ cup stock
1½ cups cooked hamburger (minced meat)
½ teaspoon mixed herbs
5-6 cooked potatoes (straight from the pot)
2 tablespoons milk
Salt and pepper

Type of Pan:

Oven-proof dish (greased)

Baking Temperature:

400°F

Baking Time:

25 minutes

Alternative Ingredient:

Before baking, sprinkle grated cheddar cheese on top.

Pikelets

by Victoria Hensen

INGREDIENTS:

1 cup all purpose flour
1 teaspoon baking powder
¼ teaspoon salt
1 egg
¼ cup sugar
¾ cup milk (approximately)

Type of Pan:

Griddle or non-stick frying pan

Alternative Ingredients:

½ cup raisins and rind of 1 orange (squeeze orange juice over when cooked)

Secret Touch:

Freezes well, in a sealed bag.

Thank God for tea! What would the world do without tea? How did I exist? I am glad I was not born before tea.

Rev. Sidney Smith

Born in Christchurch, New Zealand, Victoria is a fourth generation New Zealander: a Kiwi through-and-through. Psychologist by trade and artist by nature, Victoria and her veterinarian husband now reside in Bermuda.

For Victoria, Pikelets are a blast from the past; remembering them from home served with jam and cream.

Victoria says every Kiwi appreciates a good Pikelet. So, should any Kiwi stop by your door, you know just what to serve them!

Method:

1. Sift flour, baking powder, and salt into bowl.

2. In another bowl, beat egg and sugar until thick.

3. Add the milk to dry ingredients; mix into egg mixture until smooth.

4. Place greased griddle or non-stick frying pan over a low/medium heat on stove. With a spoon, pour small circles of batter onto pan. Turn Pikelets over when bubbles start to burst on top.

5. Cook until golden.

Makes 8 — 10 Pikelets.

Cornish Pasties

by the author — Mair Harris

Here's another recipe from the Home Economics Department's little red cookbook. When I started my career in the 1960s, I found this book invaluable and still cherish my copy, which is now brown with age, battered beyond measure but dearly held.

Method:

Pastry

1. In a mixing bowl, sift flour and salt. Cut up shortening into small pieces and rub into flour until mixture resembles breadcrumbs. Mix to a stiff consistency with water. Knead and roll out ¼" thick.

Filling

1. In a bowl, mix all ingredients.

2. Using a saucer for measurement, cut rounds of pastry. Place a portion of filling on half of pastry round. Damp edges and fold in half. Using a fork dipped in flour, or your fingers, make a neat edge; place on baking pan and brush with egg wash.

3. Make a hole in the top of each pastie and bake until golden brown.

INGREDIENTS:

Shortcrust Pastry

1½ cups all purpose flour
¼ teaspoon salt
¼ cup butter
¼ cup shortening
Cold water to mix

Filling

½ cup cooked minced meat (hamburger)
⅓ cup cooked diced potato
1 small or medium cooked diced onion
⅓ cup cooked vegetables
¼ cup gravy
Salt and pepper

Type of Pan:

Baking pan

Baking Temperature:

450°F

Baking Time:

20 — 30 minutes

Anecdote:

Cornish miners' housewives developed Cornish Pasties for their husbands' lunch. The pastry wrapping made it easy for the miners to grip this substantial meal of meat, potatoes and onions between their hands. The wives would bring them to the mine and drop them, still warm, down the dark mine shafts to their husbands. Nowadays, Cornwall is a tourist area, where it seems every other shop sells pasties of all flavours -- from curried to vegetarian -- although the original ones remain the favourite.

Welsh Rarebit

by John Jones

INGREDIENTS:

2 tablespoons margarine
1 tablespoon all purpose
   flour
1 teaspoon ready-made
   mustard
3 tablespoons beer
1 tablespoons Worcestershire
   Sauce
2 cups grated Cheddar
   cheese
4 — 6 slices of bread,
   depending on loaf size

Type of Pan:

Pan for broiling

Alternative Ingredients:

Gouda or Edam cheese
makes a creamy version.
Place ham under cheese for a
York Rabbit. Topped with a
poached egg it becomes a
Buck Rabbit.

John was born in Wales and is a keen gardener, cook and wine connoisseur, who, on special occasions, treats his Bermudian family to four or five-course dinners.

Although John uses this recipe as a savoury course at dinner parties, it is most widely known as a quick, satisfying high tea dish.

Method:

1. Melt margarine over a low heat and stir in flour with a wooden spoon.

2. Add rest of ingredients; stir until melted.

3. Using a broiler, toast bread on one side; remove from broiler.

4. Spread cheese mixture on top of each slice and return to broiler until bubbles appear and dish turns a little brown.

5. Serve whole; shake a little paprika on top, if wished, and decorate with a little parsley.

Cod Fish Cakes

by Fred Ming

Fred is probably the best known Bermudian chef, completing his studies at Bermuda's hotel college, Stonington, as well as in England. He has worked on the cruise ships and at the famous Savoy Hotel in London. Eager to pass on his knowledge to upcoming Bermudian chefs, Fred has taught at Stonington since 1973.

He has won many awards and medals in his culinary field.

Method:

1. In a pot or container, soak fish in cold water overnight.

2. Drain; add fresh water to pot and cook for ½ hour. Half way through cooking, add peeled potatoes, cut into chunks, and finish cooking with fish until potatoes are cooked through.

3. Drain fish and potatoes in a colander.

4. Using a potato masher, mash together well; add butter, onion, egg yolk and seasonings.

5. With an ice-cream scoop, scoop out round shapes and roll in seasoned flour.

6. Let fish cakes fry for 2 minutes on each side, or until golden brown.

Serves 2 dozen.

INGREDIENTS:

2 lb. salted codfish (boneless)
4 lb. potatoes (peeled)
1 onion finely chopped
1 egg yolk
1 oz. butter
Thyme and chopped parsley to taste
Salt and pepper to taste
Pinch curry powder
Flour for coating
Cooking oil for frying

Type of Pan:

Frying pan

Alternative:

Mixture can be moulded into small balls (size of a walnut) and served as hors-d'oeuvres, accompanied with a slice of ripe banana.

Banana Chutney

by Kathleen Tatum

INGREDIENTS:

1lb. chopped onions
8 sliced bananas
½ lb. chopped dates
1½ cups vinegar
2 teaspoons ginger (green or
    ground)
¼ cup raisins
1 teaspoon curry powder
2 cups water
1 cup sugar

Type of Pan:

Large cooking pot

Secret Touch:

To decorate for a gift: Take a scrap of fabric and with pinking shears, cut a circle 1" larger than top of bottle. Place on top of bottle and secure with an elastic band. Tie round a coloured ribbon.

Chutney, piccalilli, and pickled onions are very much a part of eating high tea. Kathleen brings us this easy recipe for Banana Chutney, an island favourite. Decoratively packaged, it also makes an excellent dinner party gift for your hostess.

Method:

1. In a large pot, bring the first 4 ingredients to a boil; add rest of ingredients and simmer uncovered until thickened.

2. Bottle and seal.

Pickled Onions

by the author — Mair Harris

In Bermuda, an onion has two meanings: the first being the root vegetable, which was grown in Bermuda and exported to North America from the mid-1800s to the early 1900s, and the second is a colloquial term meaning a born Bermudian.

Pickled onions, mixed pickles, or piccalilli are typical accompaniments to a high tea. This recipe for Pickled Onions has been taken from the *Bermuda School of Home Economics Cookery Book*, now out of print.

Method:

1. In a pot, cover onions with boiling water and allow to stand for 5 minutes.

2. Drain; cover with cold water and peel.

3. Make brine by mixing salt and cold water. Add onions and soak for 24 hours.

4. Drain and rinse well.

5. Pack onions into jars, placing spices in between.

6. Heat vinegar and sugar until boiling. Fill sterilised jars to cover onions; seal at once.

INGREDIENTS:

4 quarts small onions
1 cup salt
6 cups cold water
Spices: cloves, allspice, hot peppers
2 quarts vinegar
½ cup sugar

Type of Pan:

Large cooking pot

Secret Touch:

Make sure jars are properly sterilised, using your favourite method. Do not use metal tops, unless protected from the vinegar, as they may corrode.

Anecdote:

To see perfect specimens of sweet Bermuda onions, visit the annual Agricultural Exhibition, or "Ag. Show", as it's known locally. Held each April at the Botanical Gardens, it is considered such an important local event that school children are given a day off to attend.

Loquat Upside-Down Cake

by Mrs. W. E. S. Zuill

INGREDIENTS:

Topping

¼ cup butter
1 cup brown sugar
2 cups drained loquats
(stoned, cooked and boiled
until tender in a little
water)

Batter

3 egg yolks
1 cup sugar
5 tablespoons juice from
loquats
1 cup all purpose flour
1 teaspoon baking powder
3 egg whites

Type of Pan:

9"x9"x2" cake pan
(greased)

Baking Temperature:

350°F

Baking Time:

45 minutes

Alternative Ingredients:

To show you how old this recipe book is, another recipe for Jelly Babies asks the cook to grease a jelly mould with lard using a chicken feather!

This recipe is from an old, well-used cookbook, printed many years ago as a fund-raiser for a local church. In its original form, this cake was cooked in the oven in a heavy frying pan. We have updated the frying pan to ovenware you may be more familiar with.

Method:

Topping

1. In a pot, melt the butter; add brown sugar, stirring continually until blended.

2. Pour into greased pan.

3. Spread loquats evenly over mixture.

Batter

1. In a mixing bowl, beat egg yolks; add sugar, loquat juice, flour and baking powder, stirring after each addition.

2. In a separate bowl, beat egg whites until peaks form; fold into batter. Pour batter into pan and bake.

3. When baked, turn immediately onto a plate (if serving warm) or a rack to cool (if serving cold). Serve with whipped cream.

Seredipi-tea,
Tranquili-tea,
Hospitali-tea,
all good things
end in tea.

Tea and Thee
Robin Sigley

9

Especially for Kids

*After school tea-time used to consist of sandwiches, cakes, and cookies.
Nowadays, our children may well be looking for a microwave pizza, chicken nuggets,
or chips and dip. For hungry after school appetites or lunch box treats, these fun
recipes that your children can make, or help to make, fill hungry tummies
and create happy faces.*

Rock Buns 108

Raspberry Buns 109

Crunchie Chocolate
Fudge Brownies 110

Candy Pizza 111

Mini M&M Gems 112

Cheese Straws 113

Chocolate Chip
Oatmeal Cookies 114

Gingerbread People 115

INGREDIENTS:

1 cup all purpose flour
¾ teaspoon baking powder
Pinch of salt
¼ cup margarine
2 tablespoons sugar
¼ cup raisins
1 egg
¼ cup milk
1 — 3 tablespoons water

Type of Pan:

Cookie sheet
(greased)

Baking Temperature:
325°F

Baking Time:
15 minutes

"Take some more tea,"
the March Hare said
to Alice very earnestly.

"I have had nothing
yet," Alice replied in
an offended tone, "so I
can't take any more."

"You mean you can't
take any less," said
the Hatter. "It's very
easy to take more
than nothing."

Alice in Wonderland
Lewis Carroll.

Rock Buns
by Judy Ratteray

This simple and satisfying bun recipe has been used "forever" in Bermuda's schools as a good introduction to the "rubbing-in" method. Invariably, the buns never get as far as home — maybe not even as far as the bus — as they are eaten ravenously by fellow students.

Method:

1. Preheat oven, grease cookie sheet.

2. Sieve flour, baking power, and salt into a bowl. Rub in margarine until mixture resembles breadcrumbs. Stir in sugar and raisins.

3. In a separate bowl, beat egg lightly with milk; add to mixture using a spoon to stir. If necessary, add a little water. Mixture should be lumpy.

4. Scoop 8 heaps onto cookie sheet and bake until light and firm. Cool on cooling rack.

Raspberry Buns

by Ann Coakley

Ann is a teacher who gave me her version of a Raspberry Bun. At one school, I was asked to teach an after school hobby group — Ann's recipe was a firm favourite that could be made in the short time I was allotted.

Method:

1. Preheat oven, grease cookie sheet.

2. Sift dry ingredients into a bowl. Rub in margarine until mixture resembles fine breadcrumbs.

3. In a small bowl, beat egg with milk; gradually add to mixture. Using a round bladed knife, mix to a soft dough.

4. Turn onto a floured surface and cut into 12 pieces. Shape each piece into a smooth circle.

5. Make a hollow in centre of each and fill with a little jam. Sprinkle with sugar.

6. Place on cookie sheet and bake until light brown and firm to touch.

INGREDIENTS:

2 cups all purpose flour
6 tablespoons sugar
2 teaspoons baking powder
¼ teaspoon salt
6 tablespoons margarine
1 egg
⅓ cup milk
Raspberry jam

Type of Pan:

Cookie sheet
(lightly greased)

Baking Temperature:

400°F

Baking Time:

10 — 15 minutes

INGREDIENTS:

½ cup butter or margarine
2 oz. unsweetened chocolate
1 cup sugar
2 eggs
1 teaspoon vanilla essence
¾ cup all purpose flour
1 cup semisweet chocolate chips

Topping

2 cups miniature marshmallows
1 cup chocolate chips
½ cup peanuts

Type of Pan:

8"x8"x2" baking pan (greased)

Baking Temperature:

350°F

Baking Time:

30 minutes

Secret Touch:

Do not over stir mixture, as it will cause brownies to rise too high and then fall.

Up above the world you fly;

Like a tea tray in the sky.

—Lewis Carroll

Crunchie Chocolate Fudge Brownies

by Sherrie, Tyler, and Eric Thomas

Bermudian, Sherrie, teaches martial arts as a hobby and her 2 boys, Tyler and Eric, have fun together in her class.

At school, Sherrie attended food and nutrition classes, which, she says, enhanced her enjoyment of cooking. Nowadays, she loves to collect cookbooks and make great desserts on Sundays, like this one, with her children.

Method:

1. Preheat oven, grease baking pan.

2. In a pot, melt butter and chocolate together on stove; remove from heat and stir in sugar.

3. In a mixing bowl, combine eggs and vanilla together; beat lightly. Add to chocolate mixture, stirring until just combined.

4. Add flour and chocolate chips.

5. Spread batter onto pan and bake.

6. Immediately after removing brownies from oven, top with marshmallows, chocolate chips and peanuts. Let cool completely; cut with a sturdy plastic knife into 12 — 16 bars.

Candy Pizza

by Janice Amaral

Bermudians, Janice and Allan, have two children, Anita and Benjamin. Before becoming a stay-at-home mom, Janice was a nursery school teacher.

Janice fondly remembers recipes from her grandmother, and says, somehow she always remembers the sweet ones. She especially likes this recipe for Candy Pizza because very young children can make it (after the hot bit is completed).

Janice says, "It doesn't matter if it looks lopsided - the children have achieved creating a dish they can eat."

Method:

1. Coat a 12" pizza pan with non-stick cooking spray (such as PAM).

2. Melt butter in a large pot; add marshmallows and stir until completely melted.

3. Remove from heat and stir in cereal until well coated. Pour into prepared pan.

4. Coat a sheet of waxed paper with non-stick cooking spray. Place on cereal mixture and press into pan, forming a 1" thick "crust" around edge. Cool completely.

5. Remove waxed paper. Melt chocolate and stir in shortening until well blended. Spread over "crust."

6. Top with candies and cut into wedges. Serve warm or cool.

INGREDIENTS:

3 tablespoons butter or margarine
1 bag marshmallows (40, regular size)
6 cups Rice Krispies
1 tablespoon shortening
1½ cups milk chocolate chips (melted)

Toppings

Assorted candies: Dolly Mixtures, Gummy Bears, Smarties, etc.

Type of Pan:

12" pizza pan

Alternative Ingredients:

Use semi-sweet chocolate instead of milk chocolate and top with animal crackers or cookies.

Secret Touch:

For chocolate decadence, drizzle melted milk chocolate and melted white chocolate over top.

INGREDIENTS:

2¼ cups all purpose flour
1 teaspoon baking soda
½ teaspoon salt
1 cup butter
¾ cup brown sugar
¾ cup white sugar
1 teaspoon vanilla essence
2 eggs (beaten)
½ cup chopped walnuts
½ cup raisins
2 packs Mini M&Ms

Type of Pan:

Cookie sheets
(ungreased)

Baking Temperature:

375°F

Baking Time:

10 minutes .

Alternative Ingredients:

Peanuts, rainbow chips, or
chocolate chips.

Secret Touch:

Made with love, served with
kindness.

Mini M&M Gems
by Karen Edwards

For over a decade, Karen has taught three-year-olds at the Playmate Hi Pre-school in her native Parish of Pembroke. "I love working with children because no two days are alike," she says. "It is as much a learning experience for me as for them."

With energy left over after a busy day, Karen changes hat and uses her talents as a men's barber!

Karen says this recipe for Mini M&M Gems was an experiment, and the children at her pre-school love them.

Method:

1. Preheat oven.

2. In a bowl, mix together flour, baking soda, and salt.

3. In a mixing bowl, beat softened butter and sugars until light and fluffy; add vanilla and eggs. Fold in the flour mixture.

4. Stir in nuts, raisins, and M&Ms.

5. Drop ½ teaspoonfuls of mixture onto cookie sheets and bake.

Makes 6 dozen or more, depending on size.

Cheese Straws

by "Meet-a-Mum"

In 1986, the Meet-a-Mum (MaMa) group —
a support group for new mothers — was
formed, and is based on the British
forerunner of the same name.

Children love cheese straws as a snack,
either by themselves or to dip in pizza
sauce or different dips. This recipe is taken
from MaMa's Cookbook, a local publication
designed: "To allow a family to spend more
time communicating and less time rushing
around making meals."

Method:

1. Preheat oven, lightly grease pan.

2. In a mixing bowl, rub together flour and
   butter until crumbly; add cheese.

3. In a separate bowl, blend together
   mustard and milk; add to mixture above.

4. On a floured surface, roll out to about
   ¼" thickness. Cut into strips about 1"
   wide and 4" long. Sprinkle with mustard
   seeds.

5. Bake until golden brown. Eat warm or
   cold.

INGREDIENTS:

2 cups all purpose flour
½ cup butter
1 cup strong cheddar
   cheese (grated)
1 teaspoon Dijon mustard
8 tablespoons milk
Mustard seeds for garnish
   (if wished)

Type of Pan:

Cookie sheet
(lightly greased)

Baking Temperature:

350°F

Baking Time:

15 — 20 minutes

Alternative Ingredient:

Instead of mustard, add a
pinch of cayenne.

Secret Touch:

For a fun shape, try
twisting straws before
placing on cookie sheet.

Anecdote:

Taken from MaMa's
Cookbook: "Walks and
talks we have with our
two-year-old, have a great
deal to do with values
they will cherish as
adults".

— *Edith F. Hunter*

113

Chocolate Chip Oatmeal Cookies

by Reta Murdock

INGREDIENTS:

½ cup white sugar
½ cup brown sugar
½ cup butter or margarine
1 egg (beaten)
½ teaspoon vanilla essence
1 cup all purpose flour
½ teaspoon baking powder
½ teaspoon salt
1 cup oatmeal
1 cup chocolate chips
½ cup coconut

Type of Pan:

Cookie sheet

Baking Temperature:

350°F

Baking Time:

10 minutes

Anecdote:

Try a soothing oatmeal & lavender bath. A few drops of lavender and oatmeal tied up in muslin can be used to invigorate the skin.

Reta was born and raised in "Anne of Green Gables" land — Prince Edward Island, Canada. She now combines her busy life as wife of a clergyman with working in the Recovery Unit at the local hospital, King Edward VII Memorial.

With their three children grown and living off the Island, Reta and her husband are into, "exercise and healthy eating." This recipe for Chocolate Chip Oatmeal Cookies is a real treat.

Method:

1. Preheat oven.

2. In a mixing bowl, cream together sugars and butter.

3. Add beaten egg and vanilla.

4. Stir in remaining ingredients (makes a thick mixture).

5. Drop by teaspoonfuls onto cookie sheet and bake.

Makes 40 — 45, depending on size.

Gingerbread People

by Kara Harris

Kara is my daughter, and since she was small she has helped me bake boxes of variety cookies for family friends at Christmas time. Taking days to bake and hours putting the boxes together, it has become a traditional family affair.

On Christmas Eve we take part in a small private service at the ancient Heydon chapel, and after the service the nuns always produce baskets of gingerbread people, a firm favourite with the children.

Kara shares this recipe, full of Christmas memories, to enjoy with your family throughout the year.

Method:

1. Using an electric mixer, beat margarine and sugar until creamy.

2. Beat in molasses.

3. Sift in the remaining ingredients and stir.

4. Cut dough in half and flatten out onto waxed paper. Cover with more waxed paper or Saran wrap and chill for a couple of hours.

5. After cooling, take each piece of gingerbread out of waxed paper and, on a lightly floured surface, roll out to ¼" thick. Preheat oven.

6. Dipping your cutter into flour, cut out gingerbread men shapes and place on cookie sheet.

7. Decorate with currants for eyes, nose, mouth and buttons.

8. Bake. Cool on a rack.

INGREDIENTS:

1 cup margarine
1 cup brown sugar, firmly
   packed
½ cup molasses
4 cups all purpose flour
4 teaspoons ground
   ginger
1 teaspoon cinnamon
½ teaspoon nutmeg
½ teaspoon salt
½ teaspoon baking soda
Currants for decoration

Type of Pan:

Cookie sheet
(ungreased)

Baking Temperature:

350°F

Baking Time:

10 — 12 minutes

10

Coffee Lovers' Treats

This chapter has all types of coffee cakes and muffins
to enjoy with your cup of coffee.

Coffee and It's Heritage 118

Sour Cream Coffee Cake 120

Cranberry and Ginger Biscotti 122

Espresso Coffee Cake 124

Pumpkin Spice Muffins 125

Morning Glory Muffins 126

Coffee Rolls 127

Rhubarb Streusel Cake 128

Easy Hot Cross Buns 130

Karakal's Prize Winning
Applesauce Cake 131

Espresso, mocha, cafè latte, cafè au lait, cappuccino, Brazilian, Turkish, instant, flavoured, etc., etc. Whichever way you pour it, did you know that coffee is the world's most popular beverage, employing some 20 million people in the process of its harvest, cultivation, and sale?

The name coffee derives from Caffa, a region of Abyssinia. Legend has it that an Abyssinian goat herder named Kaldi discovered his flock dancing and frolicking after eating some red berries. Following suit, he soon joined his goats' prancing. A Muslim monk happened to pass by, and partook of some of the berries. He realised this was the answer to combat drowsiness during long prayer sessions.

In 1000 AD, Ethiopian tribes in Africa, mixed ground berries with animal fat, giving them an energy rush. Around the same time, Arab traders brought it to the Arabian Peninsula where it was cultivated in Yemen, a country cradled by the Red Sea and the Gulf of Aden. It was the Arabs who harvested the coffee plant and exported it to Turkey, where, for the first time, it was roasted on an open flame and made into a drink called "qahwa" - meaning, that which prevents sleep.

In 1453, the Ottoman Turks introduced coffee to Constantinople, and the world's first coffee-shop was opened in 1475, called Kiva Han.

Coffee comes to Europe and the Americas

In 1529, a Viennese, Franz Kolschitsky, slipped through enemy lines after the Turks surrounded Vienna. The Turks lost this battle, and in their hurried departure left behind sacks of aromatic coffee beans. Kolschitsky claimed these spoils of war and opened Europe's first coffee-house. He refined and filtered the brew; the addition of sugar and cream making the drink more palatable to European tastes.

By 1600, certain Catholic Italians deemed coffee to be an evil concoction. However, Pope Clement VIII actually blessed the drink, calling it a good Christian beverage.

In Britain, coffee-houses were often called "penny universities." For the price of a penny you could grab a cup of Java and all the latest political and business news, and for two pennies -- or tuppence as it was known -- they threw in a newspaper. As usual, when something interesting was happening, women were banned, although, ironically, they could open their own coffee-houses. In 1674, King Charles II tried to ban coffee-houses, but due to a public outrage the ban lasted only 11 days. Coffee-houses flourished as places to meet, discuss politics, and trade, and it was in one such coffee-house that Lloyds of London, the world's famous insurance company, evolved.

Records show that in 1607, in the new colony of America, Captain John Smith introduced the coffee bean to Virginia. Later on, in the 1700s, a French infantry officer, Gabriel do Clieusteals, transported one single coffee plant to the Caribbean island of Martinique, where it propagated into 19 million trees within 50 years. From there, it made its way into South America. It is thought that 90% of the world's coffee plantations have spread from this one seedling!

In protest to Britain's high taxation of tea, coffee was declared America's national drink. Indeed, the U.S. would possibly still be a nation of tea drinkers if the 1773 Boston Tea Party had not swayed the citizens over to coffee, and their tea supply had not been cut off by the war of 1812. And, with a Starbucks on every city corner, America now imports 70% of the world's coffee.

Coffee in Bermuda

Bermudian shipping records dating from the 17th century show coffee imported on a regular basis from the West Indian Islands of St. Eustatius, Jamaica, Antigua, Trinidad and St. Vincent.

Well-known coffee-shops in Bermuda include Rock Island Coffee, Hamilton, and Cafè Latte, with two locations: Washington Mall (upper level), Hamilton, and at the eastern end of the Island on Water Street, St. George's.

Coffee intoxicates – without inviting the police; it excites the flow of the spirits, and awakens mental powers thought to be dead. When coffee is bad it is the wickedest thing in town, when good, the most glorious.

John Ernest McCann (1902)

INGREDIENTS:

Pastry

1 teaspoon baking soda
1 cup sour cream
½ cup butter
1 cup sugar
2 eggs and 1 teaspoon vanilla
  essence (beaten together)
1¾ cups all purpose flour
2 teaspoons baking powder

Topping

¼ cup brown sugar
¼ cup finely chopped
  walnuts or pecans
1 tablespoon cinnamon

Type of Pan:

Large loaf pan 9"x5", or 8"
square pan
(greased and floured)

Baking Temperature:

350°F

Baking Time:

45 — 50 minutes

It takes 4,000
berries to make 1kg.
(2 1/4 lbs.) coffee.

Sour Cream Coffee Cake

by Joan Williams

Joan came to Bermuda from England as a teacher of home economics. After retiring, she became Protocol Officer to one of Bermuda's Premiers, Sir John Swan. This diverse position included organising catered affairs at the Premier's official residence, Camden, as well as being involved in visits to the Island by Britain's Queen Elizabeth II, Princess Margaret, and Prime Minister, Mrs. Margaret Thatcher.

Joan was subsequently awarded the CBE for services to Bermuda.

Method:

1. Preheat oven, grease and flour cake pan.

2. In a bowl, stir baking soda into sour cream and set aside (it will increase in volume).

3. In a separate mixing bowl, cream together butter and sugar until light and fluffy.

4. Gradually beat in eggs and vanilla mixture.

5. Alternately fold in flour and baking powder with sour cream mixture.

6. In another bowl, mix sugar, nuts, and cinnamon together for topping.

7. Spread half the batter into prepared pan and sprinkle with half the topping.

8. Cover with remaining batter and sprinkle with rest of topping.

9. Bake in oven.

10. Serve with whipped cream or crème fraîche sprinkled with cinnamon sugar if desired.

Secret Touch:

Make this into a dessert by adding well-drained sliced peaches over first half of batter.

Anecdote:

Coming to Bermuda from England, Joan thought a coffee cake recipe meant it had coffee in it. She quickly realised it was a cake served with a cup of coffee!

In 16th and 17th century Turkey, anyone caught drinking tea was liable to execution.

INGREDIENTS:

2 egg whites
1 egg
1 teaspoon vanilla essence
1 tablespoon Grand Marnier
1 cup white sugar
2 cups all purpose flour
1 teaspoon baking soda
¾ cup dried cranberries
½ cup slivered crystallised
  ginger

Topping

Coarse or vanilla sugar

Type of Pan:

Large cookie sheets
(lined with parchment or
greaseproof paper)

Baking Temperature:

350°F then 250°F

Baking Time:

30 minutes then 1½ hours

*The Fins love coffee
more than any other
nation, they use 26
1/2 lbs. of coffee per
person per year.*

Cranberry and Ginger Biscotti
*by Dana Marshall
and Rock Island Coffee Shop*

Rock Island owners, Lisabet and John Outerbridge, have expanded this trendy coffee lover's cafè without losing its original charm. Catering to tourists and the business sector alike, Rock Island serves over 12 varieties of freshly roasted coffees along with tempting cakes. Their green coffee beans are imported and roasted on the premises, so you can be sure you have the best.

Method:

1. Preheat oven and line cookie sheets with parchment or greaseproof paper.

2. Gently whisk egg whites, egg, and vanilla together. Add Grand Marnier.

3. Add white sugar and stir.

4. Add flour and baking soda; stir to blend.

5. Stir in cranberries and ginger.

6. Lightly flour hands and gently knead, adding more flour if necessary.

7. Form dough into flattened logs on cookie sheets and sprinkle with coarse or vanilla sugar.

8. Bake until loaves are golden and firm to touch.

9. Remove and let cool for 10 minutes.

10. Turn oven down to 250°F.

11. Slice to desired thickness (approximately ½"); place on cookie sheet.

12. Bake again for 1½ hours, turning once. For harder Biscotti — bake in oven longer. For softer Biscotti — bake shorter time.

Alternative Ingredients:

Amaretto instead of Grand Marnier. Blueberries and almonds instead of cranberries and ginger.

Anecdote:

For a real Bermuda start to the morning, drink a mug of coffee, grab a pastry, and read a local newspaper.

Nancy Astor to Winston Churchill:

"Winston, if I were ever married to you, I'd put poison in your coffee."

~ ~ ~ ~ ~ ~ ~

Winston Churchill to Nancy Astor:

"Nancy, if you were my wife I'd drink it."

~ ~ ~ ~ ~ ~

Nancy Astor and Her Friends — E. Langhorne

123

INGREDIENTS:

12 oz. chocolate chips (semi-sweet)
4 oz. unsweetened chocolate (chopped)
1 lb. diced, unsalted butter
1 cup freshly brewed Rock Island Espresso coffee (or any strong coffee)
1 cup brown sugar
8 eggs (beaten)

Type of Pan:

9" cake pan
–spring form if possible
(lined with buttered greaseproof paper)

Baking Temperature:

350°F

Baking Time:

1 hour in oven, then chill overnight in fridge for at least 5 hours

In 1946, the Espresso coffee machine was invented in Italy, using steam from boiling water forced through coffee grounds.

Espresso Coffee Cake

by Dana Marshall of Rock Island Coffee Shop

Dana was raised on the East Coast of the U.S. among a family of bakers and sailors. Their influence led her to work as a chef on the tall ships — on both the Eastern Seaboard and in the Caribbean. For many years she worked on the Spirit of Massachusetts. Dana supported herself through college by catering and baking in New York where she met her future Bermudian husband, Andrew. This Espresso Coffee Cake is a melt-in-the-mouth experience.

Method:

1. Prepare pan and preheat oven.

2. Place all chocolate in a mixing bowl.

3. In a pan, bring butter, coffee, and sugar to the boil, stirring to dissolve sugar.

4. Add this to chocolate and whisk until smooth.

5. Cool mixture slightly and whisk in eggs.

6. Pour batter into prepared pan. Place cake pan in a roasting pan and pour enough hot water into pan to come halfway up sides of cake.

7. Bake about 1 hour or until set. Remove pan from water and chill overnight.

8. Cut around sides of pan to loosen cake. For an easy release, hold and warm pan over a low heat for 15 seconds, then invert onto a platter.

9. For entertaining, garnish with raspberries and mint and serve with freshly whipped cream.

Pumpkin Spice Muffins

by Carol Raynor

Carol and her husband, Willard, love to travel and entertain. Carol is an avid cook, always getting her family to try out the exotic recipes she brings back from her travels. She leads an active life, so any recipes need to be quick and easy. This one, for Pumpkin Spice Muffins, fits the bill.

Method:

1. Preheat oven.

2. Mix flour, brown sugar, baking powder, cinnamon, ginger, salt and allspice together in a large bowl.

3. With pastry blender, 2 knives, or fingertips, mix in butter until it resembles fine crumbs.

4. In a separate bowl, beat together egg, pumpkin, milk and vanilla until blended. Stir into flour mixture.

5. Spoon batter into lined muffin cups, dividing equally.

6. Sprinkle pecans over top of batter and bake.

INGREDIENTS:

2 cups all purpose flour
¾ cup packed light brown sugar
1 tablespoon ground cinnamon
1 teaspoon ground ginger
¾ teaspoon salt
1½ teaspoons baking powder
¼ teaspoon ground allspice
3 tablespoons butter
1 egg
¾ cup plus 2 tablespoons canned solid pack pumpkin puree (not pie filling)
⅔ cup milk
1 teaspoon vanilla essence
2 — 3 tablespoons chopped pecans

Type of Pan:

Standard or miniature muffin pans

Baking Temperature:

375°F

Baking Time:

25 minutes

Alternative Ingredients:

For a healthy alternative, use unsalted butter, ¼ cup egg substitute, ⅔ cup skimmed milk and ½ cup raisins.

Secret Touch:

Spread with a little apricot or orange preserve, and eat when still warm.

INGREDIENTS:

(A)

2 cups all purpose flour
1¼ cups sugar
2 teaspoons baking soda
2 teaspoons cinnamon
½ teaspoon salt

(B)

2 cups grated carrot
½ cup raisins
½ cup nuts
½ cup coconut
1 apple peeled and grated

(C)

3 eggs
1 cup oil
2 teaspoons vanilla essence

Type of Pan:

Muffin pans
(lined with cases)

Baking Temperature:

350°F

Baking Time:

20 minutes

*The morning cup of coffee
has an exhilaration about
which the cheering
influence of*

*the afternoon or evening
cup of tea cannot be
expected to reproduce.*

Dr. Oliver Wendell Holmes

Morning Glory Muffins

by Karen Festog

Karen came from England to work as a teacher for the Somerset School of Ballet. She was fondly known by her students as "Miss Karen," so much so, when newly married, her husband, Chris, became know as "Mr. Karen."

At Women's Fellowship luncheons, Karen would invariably bring these popular Morning Glory Muffins. They are incredibly easy to make and have tons of texture.

Method:

1. Mix (A) ingredients.

2. Add (B) ingredients to (A) mixture.

3. Beat (C) ingredients together.

4. Add (C) to (A) + (B) mixture.

5. Spoon into muffin pans, filling right to top. Bake.

Makes 12 — 14.

I SAID A PRAYER FOR YOU TODAY

I said a prayer for you today
    And know God must have heard.
I felt the answer in my heart
    Although He spoke not a word.
I didn't ask for wealth or fame
    (I knew you wouldn't mind).
I asked for priceless treasures rare
    Of a more lasting kind.

Coffee Rolls

by Hon. Jennifer M. Smith, J.P. MP.

Jennifer Smith became the first Progressive Labour Party Premier in 1998, her party having been in opposition for 30 years. Ms. Smith is a representative for her hometown of St. George and she is very much an accomplished artist as well as a politician. She kindly shares this excellent recipe.

Method:

1. Put all ingredients in group (A) into a pot on a low heat; until butter melts.

2. Set aside to cool for about 10 minutes. While it is cooling, mix together in a separate bowl, group (B).

3. Mix all ingredients of (A), (B), and (C). Then fold in (D).

4. On a lightly floured surface, knead dough. Place in a greased bowl; allow dough to rise until double in bulk.

5. Remove dough from bowl, punch down and cut in half. Roll each half into a rectangle and brush with melted butter.

6. Sprinkle on cinnamon, sugar, and raisins.

7. Roll up dough, starting at longest end and cut into 3" pieces.

8. Press pieces onto a lightly greased pan. Cover and let rise.

9. Bake.

10. Remove from oven, cool on a rack and drizzle with confectioner's sugar mixed with water, if wished.

Makes about 20 rolls.

INGREDIENTS:

(A)
½ cup milk
1 stick butter or margerine
½ cup sugar

(B)
Mix the following and set aside until bubbly:
1 packet yeast
¼ cup tepid water
1 teaspoon sugar

(C)
2 eggs and 2 egg yolks (beaten together)

(D)
4½ cups all purpose flour
Pinch of salt

Filling:

3 tablespoons margarine or butter (melted)
1 tablespoon cinnamon
⅓ cup brown sugar
⅓ cup raisins

Type of Pan:
10"x14"x2" baking pan
(lightly greased and floured)

Baking Temperature:
350°F

Baking Time:
35 minutes or until lightly browned

INGREDIENTS:

(A) Filling

¾ cup of sugar
3 tablespoons cornstarch
3 cups diced fresh rhubarb

(B)

¾ cup milk
1 tablespoon vinegar

(C)

2¼ cups all purpose flour
¾ cup sugar
¾ cup butter
½ teaspoon baking powder
½ teaspoon baking soda
½ cup finely chopped nuts

1 egg (beaten)

Type of Pan:

9" cake pan
(greased and floured)

Baking Temperature:

350°F

Baking Time:

50 minutes (approximately)

Rhubarb Streusel Cake
by Cath Hunt

Cath is a Canadian whose husband, Kean, spent some years working here for his Dad's company. Like many Canadians, they spent their honeymoon here.

Cath and Kean lived for six years in the Turks & Caicos Islands, which have close connections with Bermuda: During the 1800s, the Turks & Caicos Islands were a colony of Bermuda's! For 100 years, Bermudians sailed there for the salt raking trade.

Method:

Filling (A)

1. Combine ¾ cup of sugar with cornstarch in a medium size pot.

2. Stir in rhubarb and cook over medium heat until the mixture thickens. Set aside to cool.

Cake Batter

1. Preheat oven, grease and flour cake pan.

2. In a small bowl, combine milk and vinegar and set aside -- this is mixture (B).

3. In a mixing bowl, combine flour and sugar; rub in the butter until mixture resembles breadcrumbs. Take out ½ cup and set aside. To remaining ½ cup add baking powder, baking soda and nuts. This is now mixture (C).

4. To milk mixture (B) add egg.

5. Add (B) to dry ingredients (C). Stir until moistened and becomes a batter.

6. Spread ⅔ of this batter into the pan.

7. Add filling (A) and the remaining ⅓ of batter, drop in small spoonfuls on top of the filling.

8. Sprinkle on top the ½ cup of reserved crumb mixture and bake.

Alternative Ingredient:

Canned rhubarb may be substituted for fresh rhubarb.

Anecdote:

Although we think of rhubarb as a fruit, it does in fact belong to the sorrell family thus making it a vegetable. It is a useful addition as dietary fibre to our diet.

We shall fool Satan by baptising (coffee) and making it a truly Christian beverage.
Pope Clement VII

INGREDIENTS:

1 package of Robin Hood
   Bread and Roll Mix
¾ cup sugar
2 teaspoons allspice
2 teaspoons nutmeg
3 teaspoons cinnamon
1 — 2 cups raisins

Type of Pan:

2 baking pans
(lightly greased)

Baking Temperature:

375°F

Baking Time:

20 — 30 minutes

Alternative Ingredients:

Use half currants and half
raisins (or all currants), for a
more traditional British style.

Secret Touch:

For a quick glaze, straight
from the oven, rub over the
rolls with margarine paper.

Anecdote:

In Bermuda, the place to be
Good Friday is Horseshoe
Bay where families gather to
fly home-made and shop
bought kites. The atmosphere
is festive with competitions
and dancing.

Easy Hot Cross Buns

by Lindo's Market

I spotted this traditional Good Friday bun
in a local newspaper advertisement for
Lindo's Market. Lindo's started as a small
Mom-and-Pop store and over the years it
has grown and grown. Today, their large
modern stores are in Devonshire and
Warwick but remain a family operation.

This easy recipe for Hot Cross Buns is a
little different.

Method:

1. Preheat oven and lightly grease baking
   pans.

2. Use package as directed except step 2.

3. Add sugar, allspice, nutmeg, cinnamon
   and raisins.

4. Brush top with egg wash before baking.

Makes about 36 rolls.

Karakal's Prize Winning Applesauce Cake

by Terri Durrant

Terri is a busy working mom who still finds time to be involved in her children's school activities as well as community pursuits. Her varied talents include Chairperson of the PTA, classroom mom and constant culinary winner at Bermuda's annual Agricultural Show.

This prize-winning cake is fast and easy; a great combination for busy moms.

Method:

1. Preheat oven, grease and lightly flour pan.

2. In a pot, melt margarine over medium heat.

3. Remove from heat and blend in remaining ingredients.

4. Pour batter into pan and bake.

INGREDIENTS:

½ cup margarine
1¾ cup applesauce
2 cups all purpose flour
1 cup sugar
1 teaspoon salt
1 teaspoon soda
1 teaspoon cinnamon
½ teaspoon nutmeg
¼ teaspoon cloves

Type of Pan:

9" round pan x 2" deep
(greased and floured)

Baking Temperature:

350°F

Baking Time:

30 — 35 minutes

Alternative Ingredient:

For extra texture, add one chopped apple.

Secret Touch:

Great served warm with a little ice cream or frozen yoghurt on the side.

Carefully chosen natural fruits, herbs, and spices, picked at the peak of their flavor, make these the perfect teas to refresh, relax, and soothe your body. Bermuda relaxes with...

Lipton's Soothing Moments Herbal Tea Collection

Another Quality Brand from

Butterfield & **Vallis**
WHOLESALE DISTRIBUTORS

11

Speciality Teas

Nowadays, speciality teas to the consumer mean teas of various flavours and leaves rather than strictly from the Camellia Sinensis plant. This chapter explores some alternatives for your choosing, and contains iced teas, aromatic and spicy hot teas, fruity teas, herb teas, and even a Christmas tea.

The Tea Council 134

Iced
Iced Tea. 135
Spicy Cider Punch 135
Tea Planters Punch 136
Tea Fizz 136
Fruit Fizz 137
Apple Aperitif 137
Verandah Fruit Cup 138
Rum Cup. 138

Hot
Cardamom Tea 139
Indian Spiced Tea 139
Orange and Clove Tea 140
Ginger Tea. 140
Christmas Spiced Tea. 141

Other Recipes
Bermuda Minted Tea 142
Ruth's Russian Tea 142

The Tea Council

The Tea Council, based in London, England, is an "Independent body dedicated to promoting tea for the benefit of those who produce, sell, and enjoy tea the world over."

One of the Tea Council's offshoots is the "Guild of TeaShops." For teashops to gain membership to the Guild: "Establishments [must be those] that serve afternoon tea to the high standards desired by the Tea Council. Membership (limited to 100 teashops) is by invitation only from the Tea Council after the establishment has been judged by a professional tea taster to meet the strict membership requirements."

For any visitor to Britain, a useful guide called Best Tea Places, by Jane Pettigrew and produced annually, detail guild members as well as the awards they may have won, such as, "Tea Council Top Tea Place of the Year," or "Egon Ronay Recommended." Upon reading this guide, you may decide to take tea, as I did, in the Palm Court of the Waldorf Hotel, London, where their traditional three-course tea is served on a marble terrace amongst exotic plants with background music provided by a solo harpist. Or, you may travel to the Roman Spa in Bath and enjoy tea in their historic Pump Rooms, built in 1790, on the sight of the original Roman Baths. The Pump Rooms have been a favourite since the late 18th century when fashionable society gathered to take Bath's health-giving waters.

www.teacouncil.co.uk

tea@teacouncil.co.uk

Iced Tea

2 oz. tea-leaves
4 cups cold water

Method:

1. Steep tea-leaves in freshly drawn cold water for at least 3 hours or overnight.

2. Strain cold tea liquor off into a large pitcher and place in refrigerator.

3. For plain iced tea, pour liquor into a glass over ice cubes.

4. Sweeten if desired and serve with a slice of lemon.

Spicy Cider Punch

1 pint iced tea
2 lemons
2 cinnamon sticks
A few cloves
2½ cups sweet cider
Sugar to taste

Method:

1. Pour iced tea over sliced lemons, cinnamon, and cloves. Allow to steep for 1 hour.

2. Add cider and sugar to taste.

3. Chill. **Serves 8 — 10.**

Tea Planters Punch

2½ cups iced tea
2½ cups clear sparkling apple juice
½ cup clear lemon juice
½ cup brandy
Garnish: apple, lemon, and orange slices

Method:

1. Mix tea, apple juice, lemon juice and brandy together.

2. Chill.

3. Add sliced fruit to garnish. **Serves 12.**

Tea Fizz

2½ cups iced tea
2½ cups lemonade (such as Sprite)
½ cup lime cordial
Garnish: lime slices

Method:

1. Mix together tea, Sprite, and lime cordial.

2. Chill well.

3. Serve garnished with lime slices. **Serves 10.**

Fruit Fizz

2½ cups iced tea
1½ cups orange cordial
1 pint sparkling mineral water or soda water
Sugar to taste
Garnish: assorted sliced fruits

Method:

1. Mix tea, orange cordial and sparkling mineral water together.

2. Add sugar to taste.

3. Chill well.

4. Garnish glasses with assorted fruits.

Apple Aperitif

2½ cups iced tea
2½ cups clear sparkling apple juice
½ cup clear lemon juice
Sugar to taste
Garnish: apple slices

Method:

1. Mix tea, apple juice, and lemon juice together.

2. Add sugar to taste.

3. Chill well.

4. Garnish with apple slices. **Serves 10.**

Verandah Fruit Cup

2½ cups iced tea
2 x 6 oz. bottles ginger ale
1 cup soda water
½ cup lemon juice
½ cup orange cordial
Sugar to taste
Garnish: assorted fruits

Method:

1. Mix tea, ginger ale, soda water, lemon juice and orange cordial together.

2. Add sugar to taste.

3. Chill well.

4. Serve in glasses garnished with fruits. **Serves 10 — 12.**

Rum Cup

2½ cups iced tea
1 cup lemonade (such as Sprite)
½ cup dark rum
½ cup orange cordial
Sugar to taste
Garnish: orange slices

Method:

1. Mix tea, Sprite, rum and orange cordial together.

2. Add sugar to taste.

3. Chill well.

4. Pour into glasses over ice and garnish with orange slices. **Serves 8 — 10.**

Cardamom Tea

4 tea bags
13 split cardamom pods
4 cups boiling water
Sugar or sweetener to taste

Method:

1. Put tea bags into pot with the split cardamom pods.

2. Add 1 litre boiling water and brew for 3 minutes.

3. Strain and serve.

4. May be enjoyed with or without milk. Sugar or sweetener may be added to taste. **Serves 5.**

Indian Spiced Tea

1 tea bag
¼ teaspoon of ground mixed spice
(or a mix of cinnamon, ginger, nutmeg and cloves)
Milk

Method:

1. Brew one tea bag in ½ mug of boiling water, to which you have added the spice,

for 3 minutes.

2. While brewing, heat milk (in a pot or in the microwave).

3. Strain tea and add hot milk.

4. Add sugar or sweetener to taste. **Serves 1.**

Orange and Clove Tea

20 cloves
4 tea bags
4 cups boiling water
Garnish: orange slices

Method:

1. Place cloves into a pot and add tea bags.

2. Pour on boiling water and brew for 3 minutes.

3. Strain.

4. Add a slice of orange per cup or mug, plus sugar or sweetener if desired. Best drunk without milk.

Ginger Tea

4 tea bags
2 teaspoons chopped fresh or dried ginger
4 cups boiling water
Sugar or sweeteners

Method:

1. Place bags into a pot with ginger; add boiling water.

2. Brew 3 minutes and then strain.

3. Add sugar or sweeteners to taste.

4. Best enjoyed without milk. A slice of lemon added will make a soothing lemon and ginger drink.

Christmas Spiced Tea

4 tea bags
13 cloves
½ stick cinnamon (broken up)
½ teaspoon nutmeg
2 dessertspoons of rum
Sugar or sweetener to taste
Garnish: orange slices

Method:

1. Place tea bags, cloves, cinnamon and nutmeg in a pot.

2. Pour on boiling water and brew for 3 minutes.

3. Strain.

4. Add 2 dessertspoons of rum per mug.

5. Garnish with orange slices.

6. Sweeten, if wished, with sugar or sweetener. Best drunk without milk.

Tea, though ridiculed by those who are naturally coarse in their nervous sensibilities...will always be the favoured drink of the intellectual.

Confessions of an English Opium Eater

Thomas de Quincey (1785-1859)

Ruth's Russian Tea

Ruth Harris has been mixing this tasty, hot Russian tea beverage for years, which can make a useful Christmas gift when prettily packaged for that special friend or relative.

1 bottle Tang
1 cup of sugar
½ cup instant tea
Small package of lemonade mix
Powdered cinnamon and cloves to taste

Method:

1. Mix all ingredients together and store in your favourite drinks' container.

2. In a mug or cup, mix to preferred strength with hot water.

Bermuda Minted Tea

2 pints hot tea
1 Bermuda lemon
8 stalks wild mint
Sugar to taste
Garnish: lemon slices and mint leaves

Method:

1. Chop up lemon and place in bottom of pitcher.

2. Bruise mint leaves by rolling gently in your hands. Place in pitcher.

3. Pour over the hot tea.

4. Leave to infuse about 1 hour.

5. Strain and chill.

6. Serve over ice and lemon; garnish with a sprig of mint on top. **Serves 8.**

*Look here
steward, if this is
coffee, I want tea;
but if this is tea,
then I wish for
coffee.*

*Mr. Punch
(1902)*

DISCOVER THOSE GENTLE DAYS OF YESTERYEAR AT

Enjoy the inviting old world charm and friendly unique atmosphere of

A new tearoom with personal flair and a warm Victorian ambiance that will make your lunch or your celebration of "taking of tea" a truly memorable event!

Collectibles for sale
(SORRY, NO CREDIT CARDS)

Savour our delicious Lunch Fare
and Traditional Tea
Tues. — Sun.
12 noon – 5 p.m.

MRS T's VICTORIAN TEA ROOM
25 Middle Road
Southampton
Tel: 234-1374

Opp. Port Royal Golf Course
Next to Port Royal Esso Station

Tea Equipage

Tea equipage, an old phrase for tea accessories, was used in early advertisements. Here's a nostalgic look back at all things tea.

1. Teapot

The teapot, as we know it, originated in China from the Yxing teapot of the 1500s; the design styled on the shape of a melon. They were brought to Europe packed in tea to prevent breakage. Josiah Wedgwood and Josiah Spode were among the first manufacturers of mass-produced pots in the middle of the 18th century. Their companies and good reputations still exist today.

2. Tea Caddy

The name tea caddy originates from the Malaysian word Kati -- a measure for 1⅔ lbs. of tea. The best quality, expensive tea was kept under lock and key in the caddy and opened by the mistress of the house, who didn't trust the servants. The early wooden caddy had two compartments: one for green and the other for black tea.

3. Caddy Spoon

The caddy spoon, frequently fashioned out of silver in the shape of a shell, was used to measure loose tea.

4. Teapoy

The teapoy, named by British expatriates in India, is a small three-legged table, designed to hold tea caddies and mixing containers.

5. Teaset

In the 18th century, a full teaset was designed for 12 people and would include cups and saucers, milk jug, sugar bowl, slop bowl, spoon tray, teapot and stand, tea caddy and hot water jug.

6. China

China is the name for porcelain imported from the country of China. In 1709, Johann Bottger, in the German town of Meissen, accidentally discovered the formula for hard-paste porcelain while trying to make gold. This secret formula soon spread to the rest of Europe after a Viennese factory hired two craftsmen from Meissen. Exhibits of

Meissen and other antique porcelain can be seen at the Jacksonville, Florida, Cummer Museum of Art and Gardens and also at the Smithsonian National Museum of American History.

7. Teacup and Saucer

Early tea was supped out of bowls; however, European women found it difficult to hold the hot tea without burning their fingers, so handles were added during the 1700s. This was also the time when it was considered polite to pour tea from the cup into the saucer and sip it - a practice known as "saucering."

8. Teaspoon

As an implement was needed to stir sugar into tea, a smaller version of a tablespoon was created. During the 1800s they became quite ornate, sporting patterns and emblems on the handles.

9. Tea Strainer

While pouring tea from the teapot, a strainer laid over the cup is used to prevent loose tea-leaves going into the cup. Some strainers have a stand on which to rest them.

10. Mote Spoon

A perforated spoon used to skim loose tea leaves from the cup.

11. Tea Cosy

The tea cosy was common in British households but not, however, at grand Victorian tea parties. Made of a quilted fabric, it slips over the pot to keep the contents warm. Tea cosies today are often knitted woollen ones.

12. Sugar Sifter/Muffineer

Much like a large salt shaker, the muffineer was filled with sugar, or sugar combined with cinnamon, and used for sprinkling on hot buttered muffins.

13. Sugar Tongs

Sugar became popular as a sweetener for tea in the late 17th century. Sugar at that time came in blocks, which were broken up for use. The small pieces were stacked into a bowl, and so the tongs were invented to pick the pieces daintily up. Today, they are used for manufactured cubed sugar.

14. Infusers

The infuser is a device filled with loose tea and placed in a teapot or cup; hot water is then poured on. Infusers can be ball-shaped or egg-shaped and are made of metal or plastic.

15. Tea Tray

Used for carrying a teaset, a tea tray is a flat, wooden or metal tray with a rim.

16. Tea Trolley

A tea trolley is a two-level tray structure on wheels. The hostess prepares the trolley prior to the arrival of guests, so she can serve at her leisure. A tea lady pushing a tea trolley was once a common sight in offices and factories. Dr. David Lewis, Psychologist, said, "You could find more out about what's going on (in a company) from the tea lady than the chairman."

17. Lemon Squeezer

A fairly new invention for squeezing lemon into tea. It prevents fingers from getting sticky.

18. Tea Bag Tongs

For lifting the tea bag from the teacup, mug or pot. It is recommended that the tea bag not be squeezed, as polyphenols released can make the tea bitter.

19. Tea Towels

The Industrial Revolution began in 1733 with the first cotton mill in England. This brought about the "kitchen and glass" towel production: cloths with blue and red bands woven into them, still available today. Often the lady of the house supervised the washing of the fine china, not trusting her servants with this delicate task.

Pictorial tea towels are a relatively new fashion and often bought as a vacation memento.

Having your cake and eating it too!

Safe for Diabetics

IDEAL FOR THE WHOLE FAMILY

Splenda®
No Calorie Sweetener

MEASURES CUP FOR CUP LIKE SUGAR
Great for Cooking & Baking

IDEAL FOR THE WHOLE FAMILY

Splenda®
No Calorie Sweetener

MADE FROM SUGAR TASTES LIKE

50 INDIVIDUAL PACKETS
NET WT 1.75 OZ (50g)

GRANULAR
EQUIVALENT TO
1 LB. of SUGAR

NET WT 1.9 OZ (54g)

WHY IS SPLENDA® UNIQUE?

• Splenda® has only 2 calories per teaspoon (classified by the FDA as "no calorie"), versus 16 calories per teaspoon of sugar.

• Only "no calorie" sweetener made from sugar, so it tastes like sugar.

• No unpleasant after-taste.

• You can bake and cook with Splenda®, unlike other "no calorie" sweeteners.

• Pours, measures and cooks just like sugar.

• Safe for everyone, even diabetics.

Splenda®... The sweetener that makes ALL the things you love lower in calories and healthier for you.

Use Splenda® anywhere sugar is used - in beverages and even in cooking and baking. Splenda® is the only "no calorie" sweetener that's made from sugar, so it tastes like sugar!

Splenda®
No Calorie Sweetener

The Sweetest Way To Stay Healthy!

Tea Trivia

1. Instant Tea

Made by the evaporation, freezing or filtering of hot tea and used to make instant iced tea; often pre-mixed with sugar.

2. Decaffeinated Tea

Available since the 1980s, decaffeinated tea provides an alternative for those avoiding caffeine. There are three methods the caffeine is removed: CO_2, methylene chloride or ethyl acetate. Debates continue as to which is the best method health-wise.

3. R.T.D. (Ready to Drink) Tea

Over the past few years, the soft drink industry has marketed all manner of tea: bottled or canned, sweetened or unsweetened, still or carbonated -- the market is growing exponentially.

4. Tea Blending

To create blends, tea tasters who study this profession for five years, sample hundreds of teas each day. Most of the teas we drink are blends, for example, English Breakfast.

5. Tea Clippers

The name probably comes from fast sailing ships that "clipped" the time it took to bring tea from the Far East. First launched by the U.S. in 1845, clippers were three-masted sailing ships built for speed.

6. Clipper Races

Clippers would race back to London from China. The 1886 race had 40 clippers participating with the winner taking 99 days; a far cry from the days when it took 12-15 months for cargo ships to sail from East to West. Steamships replaced clippers, and in 1871, the last clipper race was held -- an end of an era.

7. Teashops

In 1864, the Aerated Bread Company (ABC), near London Bridge, employed an enterprising young manageress who came up with the idea of opening up the shop's backroom to the public. Here the patrons could enjoy a cup of tea and a nibble. As the idea took hold, teashops spread all over Britain.

8. Tea Break

The tea break started two hundred years ago, when employers allowed tea to be served to their workers. It was considered a controversial move, as some employers thought it might make their staff lazy. Nevertheless, by World War I, it had become standard practice to allow workers a tea break, 15-20 minutes each morning and afternoon. The habit still continues today, often employee unions negotiating the terms.

9. Tea Meetings

The 1830's temperance reformers saw tea as the salvation of hard drinkers. Tea and advice were served up at revival meetings.

10. Tipping

Early tea gardens in England had wooden boxes strategically placed around the lawns for the guest to drop a coin into for the waiter. This would make sure that the tea would arrive hot from the kitchen. "T.I.P.S." was written on these boxes and this stood for, "To Insure Prompt Service." Thus tipping became the custom.

11. Tea Museums

The Pinglin Tea Industry Museum in Taiwan, which opened in 1997 and is reputedly the largest tea museum in the world, incorporates three-dimensional simulations of traditional tea processing.

San Francisco's Japanese Tea Garden features carp ponds, waterfalls, bonsai trees and Japanese-style buildings; tea is served by Kimono clad waitresses.

Or you can follow the Freedom Trail in Boston to the Boston Tea Party Ship Museum, which has live re-enactments and a free tea shop.

Tea Museums in the British Isles: Conway in North Wales; Bovey Tracey in Devon; and East Anglia's Twining Teapot Gallery in Norwich Castle.

12. Widow Twanky

In the British Christmas pantomime, Aladdin, there is a character by the name of Widow Twanky. Twanky was the name of a green tea popular when the pantomimes were first written. Tea ships were also known as Twankys, as were the sailors. When a sailor was lost at sea, his widow became known as Widow Twanky.

13. London's Cockney Rhyming Slang

Spoken mostly by the East End (Cockney) population of London, rhyming puts a colourful spin on the English language. For instance, if I lived in London, I might say, "I'll call you on the 'dog and bone' (phone) and we can meet for a 'Rosy Lea' (cup of tea)."

Here is a sample of rhyming slang in connection to tea trivia:

Rosy Lea: cup of tea
Tea-leaf: thief
China Plate: mate
Jamjar: car
Mince Pies: eyes
Bread and Cheese: sneeze
Plates and Dishes: Mrs.
Teapot Lid: quid (pound sterling)
Teapot Lids: kids
Pork Pies: lies
Uncle Fred: bread
Stammer and Stutter: butter
Cain and Abel: table

Non-rhyming British slang:

Tea Bottle: an old maid who loves her tea
Cup of Cha: cup of tea

Join the
Tea Time Treats Club

- Newsletters
- Group Teas
- Theme Teas
- Book Orders
- Special Offers
- Discounts
- Tea Talks

teatime@northrock.bm • (441) 234-0923 • fax (441) 234-3397

Weights and Measures

This book is written using the American system of cup measurements and terms. Here are the imperial and metric equivalents. Oven temperature equivalents are also included.

1 cup butter	8 ounces	about 250 grams
1 stick butter/marg	4 ounces	about 125 grams
1 cup sugar	6½ ounces	about 200 grams
1 cup flour	4 ounces	about 125 grams
1 cup confectioner's sugar	5 ounces	about 150 grams
Liquid conversion—1cup	8 fluid ounces	250 milligrams

NOTE: *All purpose flour* (American) is *plain flour* (British). In recipes that call for leavening, if using British self-raising flour omit the baking soda/powder and salt. *Confectioner's sugar* is *icing sugar*. *Shortening* is *lard*. *1 package dried yeast* is *1 cake of fresh yeast*.

Teaspoon equivalents:

1/8 teaspoon	0.5 millilitre	
1/4 teaspoon	1 millilitre	
1/2 teaspoon	2 millilitre	
1 teaspoon	5 millilitre	
1 tablespoon	15 millilitre	
1/4 cup	2 fluid ounces	60 millilitre
1/3 cup	3 fluid ounces	90 millilitre
1/2 cup	4 fluid ounces	120 millilitre
2/3 cup	5 fluid ounces	150 millilitre
3/4 cup	6 fluid ounces	180 millilitre
1 cup	8 fluid ounces	240 millilitre
2 cups	16 fluid ounces (1 american pint)	475 millilitre
1 quart	32 fluid ounces (2 american pints)	1 litre
1/2 inch	1.27 centimetre	
1 inch	2.54 centimetre	

Note: Cups or spoon measurements should always be level, unless otherwise stated.

Oven Temperature Equivalents:

Fahrenheit Setting	Celsius Setting	Gas Setting
300°F	150°C	Gas Mark 2
325°F	160°C	Gas Mark 3
350°F	180°C	Gas Mark 4
375°F	190°C	Gas Mark 5
400°F	200°C	Gas Mark 6
425°F	220°C	Gas Mark 7
450°F	230°C	Gas Mark 8
Broil	Grill	

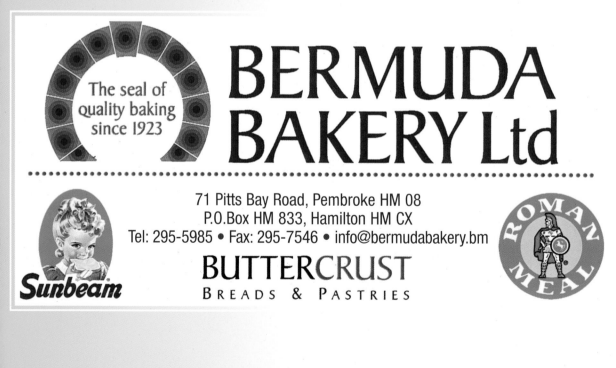

Robin Hood

Family of Flours

Bermudas Winning Choice for all your Baking Needs

Another Quality Brand from

Butterfield & Vallis
WHOLESALE DISTRIBUTORS

Index

Cookies

Almond Cookies. 77

Almond Croissants 73

ANZAC Biscuits. 57

Chocolate Chip Oatmeal Cookies 114

Chocolate Fruit Crisps 45

Coconut Macaroons 46

Coconut Shortbread. 43

Cranberry and Ginger Biscotti 122

Crunchies 58

Double Lemon Shortbread 34

Dream Bars. 26

Gingerbread People 115

Melt-in-the-Mouth Cookies 28

Mini M&M Gems 112

Molasses Ginger Cookies 56

Pecan Squares. 47

Shortbread 55

Sugar Cookies. 30

Large Cakes

Candy Pizza. 111

Carrot Cake 72

Coconut Pound Cake 60

English Sponge Cake 83

Espresso Coffee Cake 124

Hot Milk Cake. 38

Karakal's Prize Winning Applesauce Cake 131

Lemon Cake 68

Loquat Upside-Down Cake. 104

Mocha and White Chocolate Cake 70

Red Velvet Cake 53

Rhubarb Streusel Cake 128

Sour Cream Coffee Cake 120

Swiss Roll 84

Toffee Breton 74

Victoria Sandwich 82

Small Cakes

Cream Puffs 32

Chocolate Brownies 42

Crunchie Chocolate Fudge Brownies. 110

Hyacinth's Tea Cakes 29

Malassadas 62

Raspberry Buns 109

Rock Buns. 108

Welsh Cakes 54

Pastries

Auntie Joan's Iced Slices. 88

Bakewell Tarts. 86

Cheese Triangles. 96

Chocolate Eclairs 90

(Pastries cont.)

Christmas Mince Pies 91

Cornish Pasties 99

Mini White Chocolate Cheesecakes 76

Sausage Rolls 94

Scones

Blueberry Scones 52

Scones 69

Muffins

Morning Glory 126

Pumpkin Spice. 125

Breads

Banana Bread 40

Coffee Rolls 127

Easy Hot Cross Buns 130

Gingerbread 25

Irish Soda Farl 59

Johnny Bread 24

Pumpkin Loaf 39

Raisin Bread 41

Sally Lunn Buns 64

Dear friends—
Join me for tea—
teatime @ northrock. bm.

What did the world do before tea?
How did it exist? I am glad
I was not born before tea.

Sandwiches

Asparagus 79

Cheese 78

Cream Cheese and Shrimp 31

Crunchy Peanut Butter 79

Cucumber. 79

Minced Ham. 79

Open-faced Smoked Salmon . . . 79

Smoked Salmon Rollups 44

Tuna and Chopped Walnuts. . . . 78

Savoury High Tea

Cheese Straws. 113

Cod Fish Cakes 101

Pikelets 98

Scotch Eggs 95

Shepherd's Pie 97

Welsh Rarebit 100

Accompaniments

Banana Chutney 102

Pickled Onions 103

Tomato Jam 35

Animal Treats

Queen Athena's Dog Biscuits 48

Teas

Cold:

Apple Aperitif 137

Fruit Fizz 137

Iced Tea 135

Rum Cup 138

Spicy Cider Punch 135

Tea Fizz 136

Tea Planters Punch 136

Verandah Fruit Cup 138

Hot:

Cardamom Tea 139

Christmas Spiced Tea 141

Ginger Tea 140

Indian Spiced Tea 139

Orange and Clove Tea 140

Other Recipes:

Bermuda Minted Tea 142

Ruth's Russian Tea 142

The End.

Happy Cooking!

Sincerely —

Mair H.